WALKING
PARIS

WALKING
PARIS
THE BEST OF THE CITY

Pas Paschali
Brian Robinson

NATIONAL GEOGRAPHIC
Washington, D.C.

WALKING PARIS

CONTENTS

Tour Eiffel and the Seine (previous pages); rue de Rivoli (left); Notre-Dame (top right); "Venus de Milo" in the Musée du Louvre (right)

Introduction

I'm walking down the rue du Bac in the Paris neighborhood of St.-Germain-des-Prés. I'll reach the end of the street and simply, aimlessly choose a direction to walk. I don't have anywhere in particular that I must go. Eventually, I'll get to the museums and galleries and other places I've told myself I'll visit. While Paris is erecting great structures of modernity, its real charm lies in the small, the intimate, the old. Which is why I'm compelled to wander, to get as close as possible to the city's *itness*. I might linger in the Jardin des Tuileries (and if I do, I will inevitably end up at the Musée de l'Orangerie, home to Monet's seductive "Water Lilies"). And I will almost certainly linger in a café that serendipitously catches my fancy.

Paris is perhaps the world's most lustrously cinematic city. The streets seem like film sets populated by charming eccentrics, drop-dead gorgeous fashionistas, professorial types, beyond cute kids. And, while all of these can be found in other cities, add the

No. 29 avenue Rapp, near the Tour Eiffel, was designed by Jules Lavirotte and completed in 1901.

Parisian *soupçon*—dogs, thousands of them, in every shape and size—and you have a streetscape unlike any other. I do have my favorite places. Some are conventional landmarks—the Louvre, Musée d'Orsay—but many are not. More obscure treasures include the Peace Garden at UNESCO's world headquarters and the Musée du Vin in the former cellars of the Passy Abbey. And while I love to wander a city aimlessly, you may want to take more purposeful walks. This guide will be indispensable.

Keith Bellows
Former Editor in Chief, National Geographic Traveler *magazine*

Visiting Paris

Of all world capitals, Paris is the most chic. Its attractive mélange of haute couture and top-end cuisine, spectacular art collections and architectural spectacle, Gothic churches and romantic cafés, makes it—justifiably—the most visited city in the world.

Paris in a Nutshell

The Seine River divides the city into the Right Bank (Rive Droite) and Left Bank (Rive Gauche), with two islands—Île de la Cité and Île St.-Louis—sitting between. The first settlers, a Celtic tribe called the Parisii, inhabited the Île de la Cité in the third century B.C. Around 500 years later, the city was Christianized and the first churches were built. The Middle Ages saw the building of the Cathédrale de Notre-Dame de Paris and a fortress that became the Palais du Louvre.

In the 17th century, the Jardin des Tuileries and Jardin du Luxembourg were built for royal pleasure, and King Louis XIV moved the royal court from the Louvre to Versailles. In the 19th century, Napoleon I built his monumental arches and, under Napoleon III, Baron Haussmann

Paris Day-by-Day

Open every day Arc de Triomphe, La Conciergerie, Les Invalides, Musée Jacquemart-André, Musée du Luxembourg, Panthéon, Sacré-Coeur is open from 6 a.m to 10:30 p.m., Ste.-Chapelle, Tour Eiffel.

Mon. Many museums are closed except for the above and Centre Pompidou, Musée de Cluny, Musée de l'Orangerie. Musée du Luxembourg is open until 10 p.m.; Musée Jacquemart-André until 8:30 p.m. during exibitions.

Tues. National museums are closed.

Wed. Musée du Louvre is open until 9:45 p.m.

Thurs. Musée d'Art Moderne is open until 10 p.m.; Musée des Arts Décoratifs until 9 p.m; Musée d'Orsay until 9:45 p.m.; Musée du Quai Branly until 9:00 p.m.

Fri. Musée du Louvre is open until 9:45 p.m.; Petit Palais until 9 p.m.; Musée du Quai Branly until 9 p.m.

Sat. Musée du Louvre is open until 9:45 p.m. on the first Saturday of the month; Musée du Quai Branly until 9 p.m.

Sun. Most museums and attractions are open on Sunday. National museums are free on the first Sunday of the month.

Paris cafés stay open late, with people sipping drinks until well into the night.

replaced the city's maze of medieval streets with grand boulevards.

Navigating Paris

The city is divided into 20 districts (arrondissements), starting with the first arrondissement in the center and working outward in a spiral. Most maps of Paris chart the city by district and list arrondissements in the street index.

Enjoying Paris for Less

Most art galleries in Paris are free and hold *vernissages* (private viewings) on Thursday or Friday evenings, when you may even be offered a free glass of wine. For a comprehensive guide to free concerts buy a copy of *Pariscope* magazine. For a month from mid-July, the Seine's banks are converted into *plages* (beaches), complete with live music and other amusements. One weekend in October, **Nuits Blanches** (literally White Nights, meaning an all-nighter) offer dusk-till-dawn art events in buildings around the city. The **Fête de la Musique** is an annual music event on June 21 with free bands and concerts in the city's parks, concert halls, museums, and churches.

Using This Guide

The tours in this guide explore Paris's most interesting corners. Each tour is plotted on a map and has been planned to fill a day, taking into account opening hours and the times of day when sites are less crowded. Many end near restaurants, theaters, or lively night spots for evening activities.

Whirlwind Tours

Whirlwind Tours are for people who have only a day or a weekend to spend in the city and want to be sure that they see the best of the best. Choose your tour based on your time and interests: One Day; Weekend (Day 1 & Day 2); For Fun; and With Kids (Day 1 & Day 2).

Tips For the Day and Weekend Tours, a Tips spread following the itinerary map provides insider information on detours from the key sites, extra places to see, nearby cafés and restaurants, and ideas for adapting the tours to suit your interests.

Site Descriptions

In the For Fun and With Kids tours, key sites spreads following the maps provide descriptions of all the sites and practical information for visitors.

Neighborhood Tours

The nine neighborhood tours each begin with an introduction, followed by an itinerary map highlighting the key sites that make up the tour and detailed key sites descriptions. Each tour is followed by an "in-depth" spread showcasing one major site along the route, a "distinctly" Paris spread providing background information on a quintessential element of that neighborhood, and a "best of" spread that groups sites thematically.

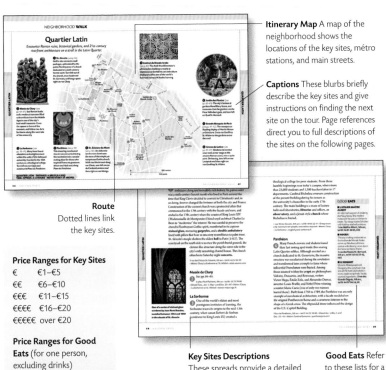

Itinerary Map A map of the neighborhood shows the locations of the key sites, métro stations, and main streets.

Captions These blurbs briefly describe the key sites and give instructions on finding the next site on the tour. Page references direct you to full descriptions of the sites on the following pages.

Route Dotted lines link the key sites.

Price Ranges for Key Sites

€	€1–€5
€€	€6–€10
€€€	€11–€15
€€€€	€16–€20
€€€€€	over €20

Price Ranges for Good Eats (for one person, excluding drinks)

€	under €25
€€	€25–€40
€€€	€40–€60
€€€€	€60–€90
€€€€€	over €90

Key Sites Descriptions These spreads provide a detailed description and highlights for each site, following the order on the map, plus each one's address, website, phone number, entrance fee, days closed, and nearest métro station.

Good Eats Refer to these lists for a selection of cafés and restaurants along the route.

PART 1

Whirlwind Tours

Paris in a Day

See the best of the city on this packed one-day tour.

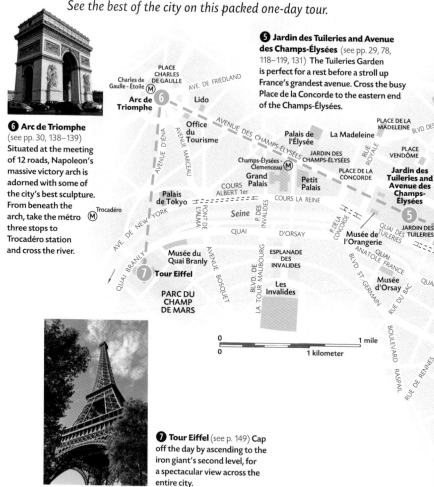

⑤ Jardin des Tuileries and Avenue des Champs-Élysées (see pp. 29, 78, 118–119, 131) The Tuileries Garden is perfect for a rest before a stroll up France's grandest avenue. Cross the busy Place de la Concorde to the eastern end of the Champs-Élysées.

⑥ Arc de Triomphe (see pp. 30, 138–139) Situated at the meeting of 12 roads, Napoleon's massive victory arch is adorned with some of the city's best sculpture. From beneath the arch, take the métro three stops to Trocadéro station and cross the river.

Map labels:
PLACE CHARLES DE GAULLE
Charles de Gaulle - Étoile Ⓜ
AVE. DE FRIEDLAND
Arc de Triomphe ⑥
Lido
Office du Tourisme
AVENUE DES CHAMPS-ÉLYSÉES
Palais de l'Élysée
La Madeleine
PLACE DE LA MADELEINE
BLVD. DES
AVENUE D'IÉNA
AVENUE MARCEAU
Champs-Élysées - Clemenceau Ⓜ
JARDIN DES CHAMPS-ÉLYSÉES
RUE ROYALE
PLACE VENDÔME
Grand Palais
Petit Palais
PLACE DE LA CONCORDE
Jardin des Tuileries and Avenue des Champs-Élysées
Palais de Tokyo
COURS ALBERT 1er
COURS LA REINE
P. DE LA CONCORDE
QUAI DES TUILERIES
JARDIN DES TUILERIES
⑤
Trocadéro Ⓜ
AVE. DE NEW YORK
PONT DE L'ALMA
Seine
P. DES INVALIDES
QUAI
D'ORSAY
Musée de l'Orangerie
QUAI ANATOLE FRANCE
QUAI
QUAI DE BRANLY
Musée du Quai Branly
AVENUE BOSQUET
BLVD. DE LA TOUR MAUBOURG
ESPLANADE DES INVALIDES
BLVD. ST-GERMAIN
Musée d'Orsay
RUE DU BAC
⑦ Tour Eiffel
Les Invalides
PARC DU CHAMP DE MARS
BOULEVARD RASPAIL
RUE DE RENNES

0 — 1 mile
0 — 1 kilometer

⑦ Tour Eiffel (see p. 149) Cap off the day by ascending to the iron giant's second level, for a spectacular view across the entire city.

PARIS IN A DAY   DISTANCE: 4.8 MILES (7.7 KM)
TIME: APPROX. 9 HOURS   MÉTRO START: CITÉ

④ Musée du Louvre
(see pp. 122–125) Skip the crowds around the "Mona Lisa" and head to the "Winged Victory," one of antiquity's greatest sculptures (Escalier Deru, Ground Floor, Denon Wing). Head west, past the Arc de Triomphe du Carrousel toward the formal gardens.

③ Boulevard St.-Germain
(see pp. 16–17, 26) Do like Pablo Picasso, Jean-Paul Sartre, and Simone de Beauvoir and dine at one of the trio of celebrated cafés along the Left Bank's moody boulevard—Brasserie Lipp, Café de Flore, or Les Deux Magots. Follow rue Bonaparte and Quai Malaquais, then cross Pont du Carrousel to the north side of the Seine River.

② Musée de Cluny (see pp. 64–65) This museum of the Middle Ages is home to some of the world's finest medieval art. The Roman baths are also worth a look. Head west out of the museum, and then take a right onto boulevard St.-Michel.

① Cathédrale de Notre-Dame de Paris (see pp. 48–49) Both a religious mecca and cultural icon, this Gothic cathedral looms above the Île de la Cité and the Seine River, still magnificent despite the damages caused by a violent fire in April 2019. From the square in front of Notre-Dame, cross the Petit Pont bridge and move down rue St.-Jacques to rue du Sommerard.

Tips

Few cities have so many world-class museums, majestic monuments, and beautiful gardens packed into such a compact area, which makes Paris ideal for anyone with only a day to spare. Yet if time is short, you may wish to customize your time with these excellent, and less crowded, alternatives.

WHIRLWIND TOURS

❶ **Cathédrale de Notre-Dame de Paris** (see pp. 48–49) Unfortunately, following the fire on April 15, 2019, Notre-Dame's fine Gothic architecture can currently be admired only from the outside. So why not dedicate some time to exploring the Île de la Cité? Stroll around the ■ **ANCIEN CLOÎTRE QUARTIER** (see p. 46), a warren of old streets north of the cathedral, to imagine the island during its medieval heyday. The ■ **MARCHÉ AUX FLEURS** (see pp. 45–46), a fabulous and fragrant year-round flower market, makes a colorful excursion. On Sundays, some of the flower stalls make way for the sale of caged birds.

❷ **Musée de Cluny** (see pp. 64–65) After exploring this medieval museum, and if you like your history on the dark side, check out the nearby ■ **MUSÉE DE LA PRÉFECTURE DE POLICE** (*4 rue de la Montagne Ste.-Geneviève, 5th arr., tel 01 44 41 52 50, closed Sun. and public holidays*), with its displays on the city's criminality and police force from medieval times to today, including a display of weaponry and a revolution-era guillotine.

❸ **Boulevard St.-Germain** If lunch at one of boulevard St.-Germain's legendary cafés, such as Les Deux Magots (see p. 158) and Café de Flore

Today, you're more likely to find tourists than philosophers at Les Deux Magots.

(see p. 158), doesn't take your fancy, try ■ **RUE DE BUCI** *(6th arr.)* instead. This foodie street offers a good range of fruit and vegetable stalls, brasseries, cafés, and restaurants from which to choose.

❹ Musée du Louvre (see pp. 122–125) This palace rivals all other Paris buildings in beauty. If you can't face the crowds (or the lines to get in), it's still worth wandering around the outside of the building to enjoy its elegant exterior. Look for mid-17th-century architect Claude Perrault's ■ **COLONNADE** on the easternmost facade, whose columns are a masterpiece of baroque architecture.

❺ Jardin des Tuileries and Avenue des Champs-Élysées (see pp. 118–119, 131) If you're walking through the Tuileries Garden during summer, make some time to enjoy the ■ **FÊTE FORAINE** *(tel 06 63 70 28 22, open July–Aug.).* Its 60 or more fairground attractions include a merry-go-round, bumper cars, and a Ferris wheel that gives great views of the Louvre. Walk up the ■ **CHAMPS-ÉLYSÉES**, which has broad sidewalks shaded by trees and lined with cafés, restaurants, car showrooms, and other stores. If you want to avoid the crowds, head a little farther north to the peaceful ■ **JARDIN DES CHAMPS-ÉLYSÉES**, which has many statues, fountains, flowers, and benches.

CUSTOMIZING **YOUR DAY**

After your day's tour, take in some of Paris's celebrated nightlife. Immortalized by artists such as Henri de Toulouse-Lautrec, the **Moulin Rouge** (see p. 171) nightclub continues to sizzle after 120 years in show biz. Check out *timeout.com/paris* or *gogocityguides.com /paris* for reviews and listings of clubs, bars, and theaters.

❻ Arc de Triomphe (see pp. 138–139) Contemporary art enthusiasts can walk down avenue d'Iéna to the ■ **PALAIS DE TOKYO** *(13 ave. du Président Wilson, 16th arr., tel 01 47 23 51 01, closed Mon., €€€, palaisdetokyo. com),* a vast art deco building that hosts shows of sculpture and installation art.

❼ Tour Eiffel (see p. 149) There is no alternative to this Parisian symbol nearby, but you can beat the lines by booking tickets in advance *(toureiffel. paris).* Brace yourself for the experience of walking on the glass floor installed on the tower's first level, 187 feet (57 m) above the city. If you wish only to look up at the tower from the ground, use the time you save to head to ■ **AVENUE RAPP,** less than 0.6 miles (1 km) to the east of the tower. The doorway of No. 29, designed by architect Jules Lavirotte in 1901, is decorated in art nouveau style.

Paris in a Weekend

The Rive Droite (Right Bank) is the focus of the first day of your Parisian adventure, from the stately Louvre to artsy Montmartre.

❺ Place du Tertre and Montmartre's Streets (see pp. 164–166) Get your portrait done at Place du Tertre or wander around this artsy hilltop hangout.

AVE DE CLICHY

AVE DE ST.-OUEN

RUE DE CLICHY

BOULEVARD DES BATIGNOLLES

Musée Cernuschi

Gare St.-Lazare

RUE D'AMSTERDAM

St.-Augustin

RUE DE LA PÉPINIÈRE

RUE DU HAVRE

RUE TRONCHET

BOULEVARD HAUSSMANN

BLVD. DES

PLACE VENDÔME

Musée de l'Orangerie

RUE

JARDIN DES TUILERIES

❶ Musée du Louvre (see pp. 122–125) Not only can you explore this Renaissance palace, but you can also see the remains of the medieval castle it was built on. Head east along the river and cross over on Pont Notre-Dame.

Musée d'Orsay

QUAI

RUE DU BAC

PARIS IN A WEEKEND DAY 1   DISTANCE: 4 MILES (6.4 KM)
TIME: APPROX. 9 HOURS   MÉTRO START: PALAIS-ROYAL – MUSÉE DU LOUVRE

4 Basilique du Sacré-Coeur (see pp. 168–169) The terraces in front of the basilica offer one of Paris's most spectacular views. If you wish, ascend the church's teardrop-shaped dome for an even higher vantage point. Head west along parvis du Sacré-Coeur toward rue du Cardinal Guibert and the warren of streets that comprise Montmartre.

3 Centre Pompidou (see pp. 90–91) The Pompidou Center's colorful exterior rises above the Right Bank's ancient mansions. Walk west along rue Rambuteau to Les Halles station, take the M4 métro (direction Clignancourt) to Barbès – Rochechouart, walk west to the base of the hill and take the funicular railway.

2 Cathédrale de Notre-Dame de Paris (see pp. 48–49) Paris's medieval cathedral was fully refurbished in the 19th century following centuries of neglect and, during the revolution, destruction. After the fire in April 2019, it is hurting once again and is currently closed for repairs. Retrace your steps across the Pont Notre-Dame and head north along rue St.-Martin.

Paris in a Weekend

Paradigms of 19th-century Paris—Impressionist art, the Arc de Triomphe, the Tour Eiffel, and café society—highlight your weekend's second day.

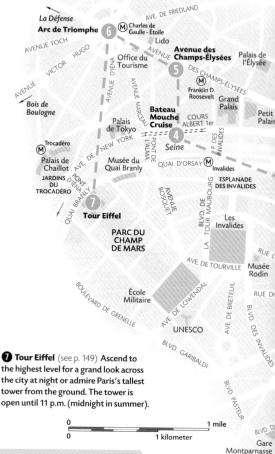

4 Bateau Mouche Cruise
(see p. 23) Catch a boat along the Seine River, boarding from between the Invalides and Alma bridges. Cruises last about 1.25 hours. After disembarking, head east along the river, then north up avenue Franklin D. Roosevelt.

5 Avenue des Champs-Élysées
(see p. 131) Take an early evening stroll heading west along France's most famous thoroughfare, window shopping along the way and taking in the tree-lined avenue's electric atmosphere.

6 Arc de Triomphe (see pp. 138–139)
Make your way to the roof of Napoleon's massive arch for a look across a Parisian evening. Take the métro from Charles de Gaulle – Étoile to Trocadéro, walk through the gardens and across the Pont d'Iéna.

7 Tour Eiffel (see p. 149) Ascend to the highest level for a grand look across the city at night or admire Paris's tallest tower from the ground. The tower is open until 11 p.m. (midnight in summer).

**PARIS IN A WEEKEND DAY 2   DISTANCE: 5.4 MILES (8.7 KM)
TIME: APPROX. 9 HOURS   MÉTRO START: CLUNY – LA SORBONNE**

WHIRLWIND TOURS

❸ Musée d'Orsay (see pp. 154–155)
It's hard to decide what is more
spectacular, the restored beaux arts
railway station or the 19th-century
art within. Head west on Quai Anatole
France, following the river to Pont de
l'Alma, then cross to the north bank.

❷ Boulevard St.-Germain (see
pp. 16–17, 26) Once frequented by
existentialists, the area is now known
for its plush shops and art galleries.
Turn right on rue du Bac, then head
west along Quai Anatole France and
the Seine River.

❶ Musée de Cluny (see pp. 64–65)
Check out some of the world's finest
15th-century tapestries, such as "The
Lady and the Unicorn," in Room 13.
Turn west on rue du Sommerard
and then turn right onto boulevard
St.-Michel.

Tips

Two days in the French capital affords enough time to see all of the city's main sites, including plenty of world-class art and architecture, as well as a few impressive smaller attractions. Use these tips to customize your weekend, and watch for some of the lesser-known sites along your way.

WHIRLWIND TOURS

DAY 1

❶ Musée du Louvre (see pp. 122–125) If the Louvre is too daunting for you, visit the ▪ **Musée de l'Orangerie** (see pp. 119–120), which displays its art, including Monet's paintings of water lilies, in an intimate atmosphere.

❷ Cathédrale de Notre-Dame de Paris (see pp. 48–49) After taking in the damaged architecture of the city's

Square Jean XXIII is a good place to relax.

famous medieval cathedral, take time to admire the 19th-century equine ▪ **Statue of Charlemagne**, king of the Franks in the eighth century, out front. Also look for ▪ **Point Zéro,** Paris's official center and the point from which all roads leading to the capital are measured. For some peace and reflection, head to the back of the cathedral to the ▪ **Square Jean XXIII**, which has plenty of benches shaded by lime, elm, and cherry trees.

❸ Centre Pompidou (see pp. 90–91) Before ascending the escalators to the ▪ **Musée National d'Art Moderne**, set aside an hour for lunch at one of the eateries around the cobblestone piazza. ▪ **Restaurant Dame Tartine** (*Place Igor Stravinsky, 4th arr., €€, tel 01 77 18 88 59*) tenders outdoor tables with a menu of French classics like *croque monsieur, tartines* (open-faced sandwiches), salads, and crepes. Its tables overlook the ■ **Stravinsky Fountain,** 16 pieces of water-based sculpture inspired by the composer's work. On the plaza's other side, the café-restaurant ■ **Le Cirque** *(141 rue St.-Martin, 4th arr., €€, tel 01 42 78 35 00, restaurant-le-cirque.fr)* offers French cuisine.

❺ Place du Tertre and Montmartre's Streets (see pp. 164–166)

If you're a fan of Salvador Dalí, visit the ■ **Espace Dalí Montmartre** *(11 rue Poulbot, 18th arr., tel 01 42 64 40 10, €€, daliparis.com)*, a permanent collection of 330 dramatically lit works from the surrealist painter, along with his recorded voice playing in the gallery.

DAY 2

❷ Boulevard St.-Germain

Although St.-Germain is well known for its existential philosophy, for a more materialist experience, visit the ■ **Musée du 11 Conti** *(11 quai de Conti, 6th arr., tel 01 40 46 56 66, closed Mon., Jan. 1, May 1, and Dec. 25, €€)*, the former state mint. Here you can find out about French coinage from 300 B.C.—when money first appeared in Gaul—right up to the modern day.

❸ Musée d'Orsay (see pp. 154–155)

After exploring this museum of 19th-

CUSTOMIZING **YOUR DAY**

You may want to spend a morning or afternoon at the **Palace of Versailles** (see p. 127). Louis XIV's massive château and garden is about 40 minutes by train from central Paris. From St.-Michel–Notre Dame, Champ de Mars–Tour Eiffel, or any of the other RER stations between, take a C train to Versailles–Rive Gauche. It's a short walk from the station to the palace.

century art, head next door to the ■ **Musée National de la Légion d'Honneur** *(2 rue de la Légion d'Honneur, 7th arr., tel 01 40 62 84 25, closed Mon., Tues., Jan. 1, May 1, Feast of the Ascension, Aug. 15, Nov. 1, and Dec. 24–25, legiondhonneur.fr)*, which has displays on France's highest order of merit.

❹ Bateau Mouche Cruise *(tel 01 42 25 96 10, €€€€, bateaux-mouches.fr)*

After viewing the city from the river, watch for the ■ **Flame of Liberty** (northern end of Pont d'Alma), an 11-foot-tall (3.4 m) copy of the flame that's held by New York's Statue of Liberty. The monument, donated by the *Herald Tribune* in 1989, stands above the tunnel where Diana, Princess of Wales, died in 1997. The flame became an unofficial memorial to the princess, although the city no longer allows people to leave tributes.

Paris for Fun

From sensuous sculpture to excellent shopping and foodie delights, nothing says fun as much as a day in the city of light.

WHIRLWIND TOURS

❶ Musée Rodin (see pp. 26, 152–153) An 18th-century château and its formal garden are home to Auguste Rodin's best-known sculptures. Walk down rue de Varenne toward St.-Sulpice.

❷ St.-Germain Shopping (see p. 26) Whether you prefer your fashion classic or hip, you'll find clothes and accessories galore in the streets around St.-Germain des-Prés and St.-Sulpice. Head east on boulevard St.-Germain.

**PARIS FOR FUN   DISTANCE: 3.3 MILES (5.3 KM)
TIME: APPROX. 8.5 HOURS   MÉTRO START: VARENNE**

7 Café Panis (see p. 27) While away the rest of the evening enjoying a lovely Seine view and great people-watching.

Musée du Louvre
QUAI DU LOUVRE
PONT DU CARROUSEL
PONT NEUF
La Conciergerie
Ste.-Chapelle
St.-Michel M
BLVD. DU PALAIS
M Cité
Île de la Cité
Q. DE GESVRES
VOIE GEORGES POMPIDOU
Hôtel de Ville
QUAI DE L'HÔTEL DE VILLE
Cathédrale de Notre-Dame de Paris
Maison de la Lozère
5
Shakespeare and Company
BLVD. ST.-GERMAIN
3
Le Comptoir
M Cluny - La Sorbonne
Musée de Cluny
BLVD. ST.-MICHEL
La Sorbonne
BLVD. ST.-GERMAIN
6
7 Café Panis
QUAI DE LA TOURNELLE
PONT DE SULLY
Île St.-Louis

0 ———————— 1 mile
0 ———————— 1 kilometer

6 Shakespeare and Company (see pp. 27, 67) Browse this historic bookstore, crammed with new and secondhand English-language books. Return to Quai Montebello and go east.

5 Maison de la Lozère (see p. 27) Enjoy the flavors of one of France's most rural regions at this specialty restaurant. Walk east along Quai St.-Michel and Quai Montebello.

3 Le Comptoir (see p. 26) Lunch at this simple, elegant brasserie, which has a terrace for fine days. Walk west on boulevard St.-Germain, then turn north on rue des Sts.-Pères.

4 Left Bank Antiquing (see p. 27) Explore the antique collectors' paradise in rue de Seine, rue Bonaparte, and rue Jacob. Walk east along Quai Malaquais, Quai de Conti, and Quai des Grands Augustins.

The garden of the Musée Rodin is an inspiring place to start the day.

Musée Rodin

1 A Paris gem, this spectacular museum in the 18th-century Hôtel Biron displays many of Auguste Rodin's sculptures. The garden is a delight, filled with roses, peonies, boxwoods, hydrangeas, and many famous Rodin works, including "The Thinker." The outdoor café is a good place for a coffee at the start the day.

79 rue de Varenne, 7th arr. • tel 01 44 18 61 10 • Closed Mon., Jan. 1, May 1, and Dec. 25 • €€€ • Métro: Varenne or Invalides • musee-rodin.fr

St.-Germain Shopping

2 Since the death of Yves St. Laurent, first Stefano Pilati, and now Hedi Slimane have kept **YSL** *(6 place St.-Sulpice, 6th arr.)* both chic and cutting edge. **agnès b.** *(6 and 10–12 rue du Vieux Colombier, 6th arr.)* is the place for affordable, simple, stylish fashion for the whole family. For unique pieces by French designers, including handbags, sunglasses, fashion, and art, drop into **Arty Dandy** *(1 rue de Furstemberg, 6th arr.)*. There are stylish own-label creations and other originals at **Victoire** *(1 rue Madame, 6th arr.)* or, for a trendy French handbag or scarf, stop by **Petite Mendigote** *(23 rue du Dragon, 6th arr.)*.

St.-Germain, 6th and 7th arr. • Métro: Sèvres–Babylone, St.-Sulpice, or St.-Germain-des-Prés

Le Comptoir

3 Chef Yves Camdeborde presides over this Parisian institution, which is impossible to get into on weeknights, but by day and on weekends it's a delightful and delicious brasserie *(lunch menu available until 6 p.m., weekdays)*. Fancy a simple but elegant salad of greens and foie gras and a glass of rosé? This is the place. Seating outside on the terrace is year-round, with blankets in winter.

9 carrefour de l'Odéon, 6th arr. • tel 01 44 27 07 97 • €€ • Métro: Odéon

Left Bank Antiquing

4 The area known as the **Carré Rive Gauche** is perfect for a stroll and some antique shopping. There are more than a hundred antique and art dealers selling everything from beautiful pieces of primitive art to exquisite Louis XIV furniture.

Between rue du Bac and rue des Saints-Pères, rue de l'Université and quai Voltaire • Métro: Rue du Bac or St.-Germain des-Prés • carrerivegauche.com

Maison de la Lozère

5 Take a trip to the Lozère region of southeast France—where cattle roam and Roquefort is aged—without leaving Paris. Dine on *salade au Roquefort*, hearty brown bread, and *entrecôte de Lozère* (steak) accompanied by one of the region's wines. On Thursdays, the menu includes a dreamy *aligot*, the region's famous dish of creamed potatoes with Cantal cheese, which is hard to find anywhere else in the capital.

1 bis & 4 rue Hautefeuille, 6th arr. • tel 01 43 54 26 64 • Closed Sun. and Mon. • €€ • Reservation required • Métro: St.-Michel • lozere-a-paris.com

Shakespeare and Company

6 Here is one of the most charming and bohemian English-language bookstores in the world. Countless writers have visited to browse and rest among the stacks. If you buy a book, get a cashier to emboss it with their famous "Shakespeare & Co. Kilometer Zero Paris" stamp on the way out, which makes for a great souvenir.

37 rue de la Bûcherie, 5th arr. • tel 01 43 25 40 93 • Métro: St.-Michel • shakespeareandcompany.com

Café Panis

7 Stop here for a *digestif* or a coffee while enjoying the terrace in good weather, with an excellent view of the Seine and Notre-Dame. From here you can watch rollerbladers do tricks and people wander by, or just gaze at the moon rising over Paris.

21 quai Montebello, 5th arr. • tel 01 43 54 19 71 • €€ • Métro: St.-Michel

Paris in a Weekend with Kids

Your first family day in Paris is packed with famous attractions, including one of the world's greatest art museums and the Tour Eiffel.

WHIRLWIND TOURS

5 Aquarium de Paris-Cinéaqua (see p. 30) Inside the Trocadéro Gardens is a small but certainly interesting aquarium. After the visit, just cross the river.

Charles de
Gaulle - Étoile Ⓜ

**Arc de
Triomphe** 4

PLACE
CHARLES
DE GAULLE -
ÉTOILE

AVE. VICTOR HUGO

AVENUE DIÉNA

AVENUE MARCEAU

AVENUE DES CHAMPS-ÉLYSÉES

**Avenue
des Champs-
Élysées**

3 Ⓜ Champs-Élysées -
Clemenceau

*Bois de
Boulogne*

Palais de
Chaillot

Trocadéro Ⓜ

**Aquarium
de Paris
-Cinéaqua**

5

Palais
de Tokyo

COURS
ALBERT 1er

Grand
Palais

Petit
Palais

COURS LA REINE

AVE. DE NEW YORK

PONT DE
L'ALMA

Seine

P. DES
INVALIDES

P. DE LA
CONCORDE

**JARDINS
DU
TROCADÉRO**

QUAI BRANLY

QUAI

D'ORSAY

Musée du
Quai Branly

AVENUE

BOSQUET

ESPLANADE
DES
INVALIDES

Assemblée
Nationale

Tour Eiffel

6

BLVD. DE
LA TOUR
MAUBOURG

PONT DE
BIR HAKEIM

Champ de Mars -
Tour Eiffel

Ⓜ Bir-Hakeim

**PARC DU
CHAMP
DE MARS**

Les
Invalides

Musée
Rodin

RUE

AVE. DE TOURVILLE

BOULEVARD

DE GRENELLE

École
Militaire

AVE. DE LOWENDAL

AVE. DE BRETEUIL

Hôtel
Matignon

RUE DE

AVE. DE SUFFREN

BLVD. DES INVALIDES

UNESCO

6 Tour Eiffel (see pp. 31, 149)
Climb the stairs or ride the elevator to the second floor of the iron tower to end the day with the city beneath your feet.

**PARIS WITH KIDS DAY 1   DISTANCE: 2.8 MILES (4.5 KM)
TIME: APPROX. 7 HOURS   MÉTRO START: PALAIS-ROYAL – MUSÉE DU LOUVRE**

④ Arc de Triomphe (see pp. 30, 138–139)
Napoleon's triumphal arch towers over the Étoile, the city's busiest traffic circle. Take the métro three stops to Trocadéro station. Walk southeast to the Jardins du Trocadéro

③ Avenue des Champs-Élysées (see pp. 30, 131) Take in the busy shops of Paris's most famed street and discover the Grand Palais's science museum (closed from Dec. 2020 to spring 2024). Continue west to the huge stone archway.

② Jardin des Tuileries
(see pp. 30, 118–119) Paris's oldest park is filled with statues, fountains, and a fairground in the summer months. Leave from the park's western end and cross Place de la Concorde.

① Musée du Louvre (see pp. 30, 122–125)
See the Egyptian mummies and other wonders in this famous art museum. Exit via the Carrousel entrance.

WHIRLWIND TOURS

Musée du Louvre

1 Taking your kids to such a large museum can be daunting, yet it is worth it . Head to the **Egyptian mummies** (Sully Wing) or the gory **Italian and French Renaissance paintings** (Denon Wing), before exploring the **medieval castle foundations** (Sully Wing).

Rue de Rivoli, 1st arr. • tel 01 40 20 53 17 • Closed Tues., Jan. 1, May 1, and Dec. 25; open until 9:45 p.m. Wed., Fri., and every first Sat. of the month • €€€€• Métro: Palais-Royal – Musée du Louvre • louvre.fr

SAVVY **TRAVELER**

To avoid the Louvre's long lines, use the entrance at the Palais-Royal – Musée du Louvre métro stop, rather than the main visitors' entrance.

Jardin des Tuileries

2 These gardens are a breath of fresh air after the museum; a place to picnic and run around. From June to late August, the **Fête Foraine carnival** (see p. 17) takes over part of the gardens, complete with a Ferris wheel and many other rides.

Rue de Rivoli and Place de la Concorde, 1st arr. • Métro: Tuileries

Avenue des Champs-Élysées

3 Stroll down this tree-lined street, past chic shops, restaurants, and cafés. Look for the **Disney Store** *(No. 44)* or, for some chocolate, try **Jadis et Gourmande** just off the avenue at 49 bis, avenue Franklin D. Roosevelt. The superb science museum at the **Palais de la Découverte** (see p. 135) will be closed from December 2020 until the spring of 2024 for renovation and upgrade.

Ave. des Champs-Élysées, 8th arr. • Métro: Champs-Élysées – Clemenceau

Arc de Triomphe

4 Kids, like adults, will be awed by the size of Napoleon's triumphal arch. They will also love the view from the roof and will no doubt be fascinated by the crazy Parisian traffic below.

Place Charles de Gaulle, 8th arr. • tel 01 55 37 73 77 • Closed May 8, July 14, and Nov. 11 (a.m.); Jan. 1, May 1, and Dec. 25 (all day) • €€€ • Métro: Charles de Gaulle – Étoile • arcdetriompheparis.com

WHIRLWIND TOURS

The fountains in the Louvre's courtyard are a good place to cool down on a hot day.

Aquarium de Paris-Cinéaqua

5 It has everything from Mediterranean marine fauna to colorful tropical fish, sharks, and a brand-new jellyfish zoo. In addition, there's a wide selection of recreational activities for the entire family.

Jardins du Trocadéro, 5 ave. Albert de Mun, 16th arr. • tel 01 40 69 23 23 • €€€€, children €€€ (free admission under 3) • Métro: Iéna or Trocadéro • cineaqua.com

Tour Eiffel

6 End your day at this giant iron landmark. The best views are had from the second level, but kids will probably want to test their nerves by crossing the glass floor on the level below.

Parc du Champ de Mars, 5 ave. Anatole, 7th arr. • tel 08 92 70 12 39 • To second floor and top: €€€€, €€€€€; for stairs: €€€ • Métro: Bir-Hakeim • toureiffel.paris

Paris in a Weekend with Kids

The second day of your weekend with kids is brimming with modern art, medieval cathedrals, and a fabulous park.

Basilique du Sacré-Coeur

Musée de Montmartre PLACE DU TERTRE

RUE DE MAUBEUGE

RUE LA FAYETTE

Folies Bergère

Musée Grévin

BLVD POISSONNIÈRE

RUE

❶ **Cathédrale de Notre-Dame de Paris** (see pp. 34, 48–49) From the first stone, laid in 1163, it took 180 years to build Europe's first great Gothic cathedral, whose gargoyles will leave kids spellbound. Head north on rue d'Arcole, then turn left onto Quai de la Corse along the Seine River.

❷ **La Conciergerie** (see pp. 34, 44–45) This 14th-century former royal palace was converted into a prison in 1391. To leave the Île de la Cité cross the Pont Neuf, then turn left onto Quai du Louvre and immediately right on the rue de l'Arbre Sec.

Les Halles Les Halles Ⓜ

Bourse de Commerce

PLACE DU CHÂTELET

Musée en Herbe ❸

Châtelet Ⓜ

❸ **Musée en Herbe** (see p. 31) Art becomes a game for visitors of all ages with exhibits, workshops, guided tours and special events. Please note: almost all of these activities are in French. Head east on rue de Rivoli, turn left onto boulevard de Sébastopol and then right onto rue Aubry le Boucher.

Pont Neuf Ⓜ

QUAI DE LA MÉGISSERIE

PONT NEUF

La Conciergerie ❷

QUAI DE MONTEBELLO

BLVD DU PALAIS

Ⓜ St.-Michel

Musée de Cluny

La Sorbonne

Panthéon

PARIS WITH KIDS DAY 2   DISTANCE: 4.6 MILES (7.4 KM) TIME: APPROX. 8 HOURS   MÉTRO START: CITÉ

WHIRLWIND TOURS

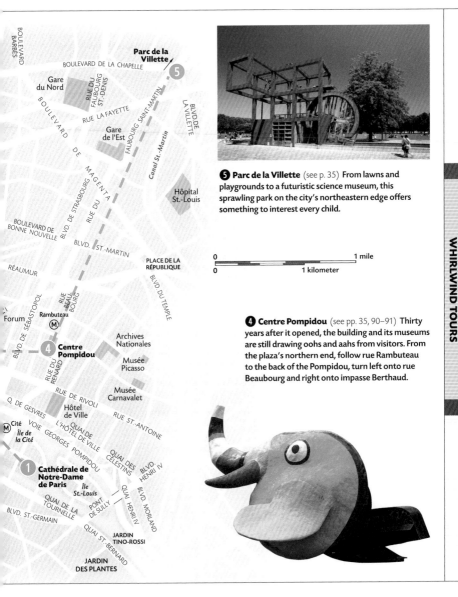

Parc de la Villette

BOULEVARD BARBÈS
BOULEVARD DE LA CHAPELLE
Gare du Nord
RUE DU FAUBOURG ST.-DENIS
RUE LA FAYETTE
BOULEVARD
Gare de l'Est
FAUBOURG SAINT-MARTIN
Canal St.-Martin
BLVD DE LA VILLETTE
DE
MAGENTA
RUE DE STRASBOURG
RUE DU
Hôpital St.-Louis
BOULEVARD DE BONNE NOUVELLE
BLVD. ST.-MARTIN
RÉAUMUR
PLACE DE LA RÉPUBLIQUE
RUE BEAUBOURG
BLVD DU TEMPLE
Forum
BLVD. DE SÉBASTOPOL
Rambuteau
Archives Nationales
Musée Picasso
Centre Pompidou
RUE DU RENARD
Musée Carnavalet
RUE DE RIVOLI
Q. DE GESVRES
Hôtel de Ville
RUE ST-ANTOINE
Cité
VOIE
L'HÔTEL DE VILLE
Île de la Cité
QUAI DE
QUAI GEORGES POMPIDOU
QUAI DES CÉLESTINS
BLVD. HENRI IV
Cathédrale de Notre-Dame de Paris
Île St.-Louis
PONT DE SULLY
QUAI HENRI IV
BLVD. MORLAND
QUAI DE LA TOURNELLE
BLVD. ST-GERMAIN
QUAI ST-BERNARD
JARDIN TINO-ROSSI
JARDIN DES PLANTES

5 **Parc de la Villette** (see p. 35) From lawns and playgrounds to a futuristic science museum, this sprawling park on the city's northeastern edge offers something to interest every child.

0 ————————————————— 1 mile
0 ————————————————— 1 kilometer

4 **Centre Pompidou** (see pp. 35, 90–91) Thirty years after it opened, the building and its museums are still drawing oohs and aahs from visitors. From the plaza's northern end, follow rue Rambuteau to the back of the Pompidou, turn left onto rue Beaubourg and right onto impasse Berthaud.

Cathédrale de Notre-Dame de Paris

1 Quasimodo, Victor Hugo's hunchbacked bell ringer, might be fictional, but the cathedral's **gargoyles** and **chimeras** are for real. Notre-Dame is currently closed to the public following the violent fire of April 2019 so, at the moment, it isn't possible to dive completely into its medieval atmosphere. But it only takes a little bit of imagination to envision Quasimodo and the beautiful gypsy, Esmeralda, hiding among the **bells** and **flying buttresses**, looking down on Paris.

6 parvis de Notre-Dame, 4th arr. • tel 01 42 34 56 10 • Closed until further notice • Métro: Cité or St.-Michel • notredamedeparis.fr

SAVVY **TRAVELER**

Paris has several permanent circuses, including the historic **Cirque d'Hiver** (*110 rue Amelot, 11th arr., tel 01 47 00 28 81, €€€€€*) near the Marais. Founded in 1852, the current shows include performing horses and tigers, magicians, acrobats, trapeze artists, and stunt bikes. And let's not forget the clowns.

La Conciergerie

2 The closest the city center comes to a medieval castle, this hulking structure was built by King Philippe the Fair in the 14th century as a royal palace, and it was later used as a notorious prison. Many who lost their heads to the guillotine during the French Revolution, including Queen Marie-Antoinette, were kept in these cold, stone cells before their deaths. Among the gruesome artifacts displayed inside are a **guillotine blade,** a **fountain** where the prisoners washed their clothes, a **stone table** where they ate, and the **Corner of the Last Good-byes,** where they boarded the tumbrel carts that took them to their execution. Needless to say, the Conciergerie is considered very haunted.

2 blvd. du Palais, 1st arr. • tel 01 53 40 60 80 • Closed May 1 and Dec. 25 • €€ • Métro: Cité or St.-Michel • paris-conciergerie.fr

Musée en Herbe

3 Open 363 days a year, the Musée en Herbe has been offering fun art shows and activities for all ages since 1975.

23 rue de l'Arbre Sec, 1st arr. • tel 01 40 67 97 66 • Closed Jan. 1 and Dec. 25 • €–€€€ • Métro: Louvre-Rivoli or Pont Neuf • museeenherbe.com

Centre Pompidou

4 Kids will be fascinated by this multicolored, inside-out building, with a facade covered in pipes, ducts, and other functional features. Much of the interior is taken up by one of Europe's most important collections of modern and contemporary art. On the ground floor, check to see if there's anything on at the **Children's Workshop**—an excellent space that holds various classes for six- to 12-year-olds. Also on the ground floor, the innovative **Galerie des Enfants** presents artistic exhibits and activities especially designed for kids. The outdoor spaces are just as dynamic: a cobblestone plaza that attracts Paris's best street performers and the **Igor Stravinsky Fountain** with its funky sculptures by artists Niki de Saint Phalle and Jean Tinguely.

Place Georges Pompidou, 4th arr. • tel 01 44 78 12 33 • Closed Tues. and May 1 • Musée National d'Art Moderne: €€€; access to Level 6 walkway: € • Métro: Rambuteau, Châtelet, or Hôtel de Ville • centrepompidou.fr

Parc de la Villette

5 Creative urban renewal morphed an ugly 19th-century industrial area into a huge green space replete with lawns, playgrounds, and themed gardens designed especially for children. The park is known for its giant abstract structures that kids are free to climb all over. On the north side of the canal that runs through the park, **La Cité des Sciences et de l'Industrie** *(30 ave. Corentin-Cariou, tel 01 85 53 99 74, closed Mon., €€€, cite-sciences.fr)* is a science museum packed with hands-on exhibits showcasing everything from space travel and natural disasters to the origins of life.

Ave. Jean Jaurès • Métro: Porte de la Villette or Pantin • lavillette.com

La Cité des Sciences et de l'Industrie has one of France's biggest movie theaters.

PART 2

Paris's Neighborhoods

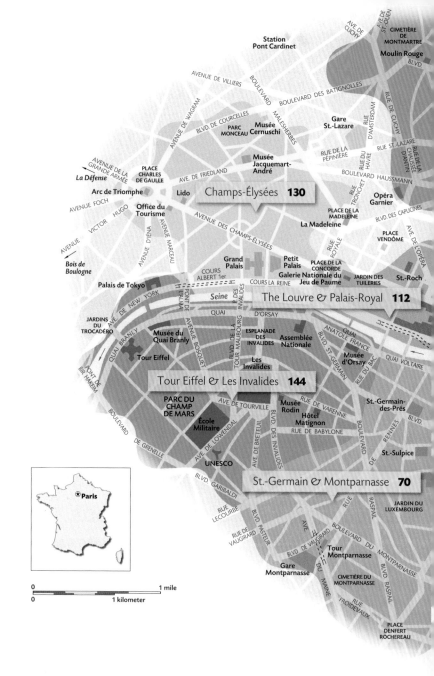

Paris's Neighborhoods

Musée de Montmartre
Basilique du Sacré-Coeur
PLACE DU TERTRE

DE CLICHY

Montmartre 160

Gare du Nord

RUE DU FAUBOURG ST.-DENIS

RUE LA FAYETTE

BLVD. DE LA VILLETTE

RUE DE MAUBEUGE

BOULEVARD

DE

MAGENTA

Gare de l'Est

Canal St.-Martin

BLVD. DE LA VILLETTE

RUE DE CHÂTEAUDUN

RUE LA FAYETTE

Folies Bergère

Hôpital St.-Louis

BLVD. MONTMARTRE

BLVD. DES ITALIENS

BLVD POISSONNIÈRE

BOULEVARD DE BONNE NOUVELLE

RUE DE STRASBOURG

RUE DU

BLVD. ST.-MARTIN

RUE DU 4 SEPTEMBRE

RUE RÉAUMUR

RUE ST.-MARTIN

BLVD. ST.-MARTIN

PLACE DE LA RÉPUBLIQUE

AVENUE DE LA RÉPUBLIQUE

PLACE DES VICTOIRES

Châtelet & Les Halles 82

Palais-Royal
Comédie Française

Les Halles
Bourse de Commerce Forum

BLVD. DE SÉBASTOPOL

RUE DU RENARD

Centre Pompidou

BOULEVARD DU TEMPLE

BOULEVARD

BOULEVARD RICHARD LENOIR

VOLTAIRE

Cimetière du Père-Lachaise

RUE DE RIVOLI

Musée du Louvre

QUAI DU LOUVRE

PONT DES ARTS

PONT NEUF

QUAI DE LA MÉGISSERIE

PLACE DU CHÂTELET

RUE DE RIVOLI

Archives Nationales

Musée Picasso

Musée de l'Histoire de France

Musée Carnavalet

Le Marais & Bastille 96

La Conciergerie
Ste.-Chapelle

Île de la Cité

Q. DE GESVRES

VOIE GEORGES

Hôtel de Ville

QUAI DE L'HÔTEL DE VILLE

POMPIDOU

QUAI DES CÉLESTINS

RUE ST.-ANTOINE

PLACE DES VOSGES

BLVD. HENRI IV

PLACE DE LA BASTILLE

RUE DU FAUBOURG ST.-ANTOINE

QUAI

DE MONTEBELLO

The Islands 40

Cathédrale de Notre-Dame de Paris

Île St.-Louis

QUAI DE LA TOURNELLE

PONT DE SULLY

QUAI HENRI IV

RUE DE LYON

AVE. LEDRU-ROLLIN

AVE. DAUMESNIL

DIDEROT

ST.-GERMAIN

Musée de Cluny

BLVD. ST.-GERMAIN

Palais du Luxembourg

La Sorbonne

BOULEVARD SAINT-MICHEL

Panthéon

Institut du Monde Arabe

JARDIN TINO-ROSSI

QUAI ST.-BERNARD

PONT D'AUSTERLITZ

QUAI MORLAND

QUAI DE LA RAPÉE

BOULEVARD

Gare de Lyon

Quartier Latin 54

JARDIN DES PLANTES

Bois de Vincennes

Grande Mosquée de Paris

Hôpital Val de Grâce

Musée National d'Histoire Naturelle

QUAI DE L'HÔPITAL

Gare d'Austerlitz

Seine

QUAI D'AUSTERLITZ

PONT DE BERCY

QUAI DE BERCY

BLVD. DE BERCY

BOULEVARD DE PORT-ROYAL

BLVD. ST.-MARCEL

BOULEVARD DE L'HÔPITAL

QUAI DE LA GARE

BLVD. ST.-JACQUES

AVE. DES GOBELINS

BOULEVARD VINCENT AURIOL

BLVD. AUGUSTE BLANQUI

PLACE D'ITALIE

The Islands

Two islands in the Seine River—the Île de la Cité and Île St.-Louis—are at the heart of Paris's 2,000-year history. It was here that a Celtic tribe called the Parisii established a fishing village that evolved into a strategic Roman town, which in turn became the seat of the French kings and a hotbed of the revolution. The evidence of this rich history remains, from Cathédrale de Notre-Dame de Paris's towers and the stained glass of Ste.-Chapelle to the bastions of the Conciergerie prison and the 17th-century mansions that housed the leading figures of the Enlightenment. That bygone vibe endures in the Gothic churches, the flower market, the narrow streets of Île St.-Louis, and the cloister quarter beside Notre-Dame, where the 21st century still seems far, far away. The Conciergerie prison may now host guided tours, rather than prisoners on their way to the guillotine, but the islands retain their real-world power in institutions like the Palais de Justice. Away from the crowds, quiet parks and quayside perches provide places to sit and relax by the river.

❶ **The medieval Cathédrale de Notre-Dame de Paris replaced an earlier Christian basilica built at least five centuries before.**

The Islands

For a flavor of Paris, stroll the length of the Îles de la Cité and St.-Louis, where little has changed in 400 years.

① Square du Vert-Galant (see p. 44) Start beneath King Henri IV's bold equestrian statue overlooking the riverfront park that bears his nickname, then walk east to the Pont Neuf bridge.

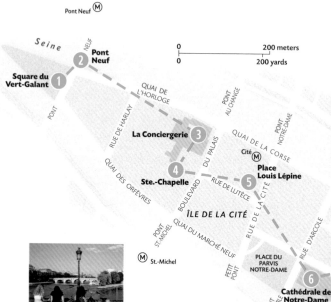

Pont Neuf Ⓜ

Seine

PONT NEUF

Pont Neuf ②

Square du Vert-Galant ①

QUAI DE L'HORLOGE

PONT

RUE DE HARLAY

QUAI DES ORFÈVRES

0 — 200 meters
0 — 200 yards

PONT AU CHANGE

La Conciergerie ③

DU PALAIS

QUAI DE LA CORSE

PONT NOTRE-DAME

Cité Ⓜ

Place Louis Lépine ⑤

Ste.-Chapelle ④

BOULEVARD

RUE DE LUTÈCE

RUE DE LA CITÉ

ÎLE DE LA CITÉ

PONT ST.-MICHEL

QUAI DU MARCHÉ NEUF

RUE D'ARCOLE

Ⓜ St.-Michel

PLACE DU PARVIS NOTRE-DAME

PETIT PONT

Cathédrale de Notre-Dame de Paris ⑥

PONT AU DOUBLE

HENRICI·MAGNI

D D

② Pont Neuf (see p. 44) The city's oldest bridge leaps the Seine River in 12 elegant arches and a patch of terra firma at the Île de la Cité's western end. Remain on the island and walk east along Quai de l'Horloge. Turn right onto boulevard du Palais.

③ La Conciergerie (see pp. 44–45) Marie-Antoinette and Robespierre were among the thousands who started their journey to the guillotine from this palace turned prison. On leaving, turn right onto boulevard du Palais.

THE ISLANDS   DISTANCE: APPROX 1.5 MILES (2.4 KM)
TIME: APPROX. 5–6 HOURS   MÉTRO START: PONT NEUF

❽ Île St.-Louis (see pp. 46–47) Now home of Berthillon ice cream and specialty shops, the aristocratic island preserves its 17th-century architecture and timeless character. Head east to explore rue St.-Louis en l'Île.

❼ Ancien Cloître Quartier (see p. 46) All that remains of the cloisters that once surrounded Notre-Dame is this tiny maze of streets along the Seine. From the park behind Notre-Dame, cross over the Pont St.-Louis.

❻ Cathédrale de Notre-Dame de Paris (see pp. 48–49) Despite the damage caused by the fire in April 2019, France's most celebrated cathedral is every bit as imposing today as 700 years ago, a structure that was meant to both inspire and instill the fear of God. From the front of the cathedral, walk a block north along rue d'Arcole.

THE ISLANDS

Ancien Cloître Quartier

⑦

QUAI AUX FLEURS

PONT D'ARCOLE

Pont Marie Ⓜ

QUAI DE BOURBON

PONT ST.-LOUIS

ÎLE ST.-LOUIS

RUE ST.-LOUIS

PONT MARIE

QUAI D'ANJOU

SQUARE JEAN XXIII

⑧

Île St.-Louis

RUE DES DEUX PONTS EN L'ÎLE

Saint-Louis-en-l'Île

PONT DE L'ARCHEVÊCHÉ

❹ Ste.-Chapelle (see p. 45) St. Louis built this Gothic masterpiece for Christian relics brought back from the Middle East during the 13th-century Crusades. Cross boulevard du Palais and walk a block down rue de Lutèce.

QUAI DE BÉTHUNE

Seine

BLVD. HENRI IV

❺ Place Louis Lépine (see pp. 45–46) A flower market rules the square on weekdays, and on Sundays an equally colorful bird market takes place. Move a block down rue de la Cité to the cathedral square and its equestrian statue of Charlemagne.

Square du Vert-Galant

1 Like the prow of a great ship, the square punctuates the downstream end of the Île de la Cité. Reached via stairs descending from street level, the leafy triangle is the only part of the island that lies at the original water level. The square is named for King Henri IV—dubbed the "Vert Galant" because of his dashing reputation as a lothario—whose **equestrian statue** is on the terrace at the top of the stairs. Legend has it that the large tree near the park's western end is the first in Paris to turn green in spring. It was here that Jacques de Molay, last grand master of the Knights Templar, was burned at the stake in 1314. Tour boats depart from the park's north shore.

15 place du Pont Neuf, 1st arr. • Métro: Pont Neuf

The Pont Neuf is popular as a thoroughfare and for enjoying views of the river.

Pont Neuf

2 Despite having a name meaning "New Bridge," this is the oldest of the city's many spans across the Seine River. Construction finished in 1607, and although restored many times, the bridge looks much the same as 400 years ago— seven arches on the north side of the island and five on the south, decorated with gargoyles and other grotesques. Pont Neuf's dreamy panoramas attract both photographers and lovers searching for the city's most romantic spot.

Île de la Cité, 1st arr. • Métro: Pont Neuf

La Conciergerie

3 In the midst of the French Revolution, the Reign of Terror (1793–1794) reached its cruelest extreme inside this notorious prison on the north shore of the Île de la Cité. Originally part of a medieval royal palace, the turreted structure was converted into a prison in the late 14th century. By the late 18th century, thousands of people were being tried, tortured, and detained inside, awaiting the executioner's blade. Queen Marie-Antoinette spent several months in captivity before her date with destiny, near the cells where revolutionary leaders Robespierre and Danton were later imprisoned before their own beheadings. The **Chapelle des Girondins**—where 22 revolutionaries spent their last night singing and dancing around the body of a dead comrade—is now a museum displaying Marie-Antoinette's crucifix and a guillotine blade, among other items.

2 blvd. du Palais, 1st arr. • tel 01 53 40 60 80 • Closed May 1 and Dec. 25
• €€ • Métro: Cité, Châtelet, or St.-Michel • paris-conciergerie.fr

Ste.-Chapelle

4 This delicate building—an exquisite former royal chapel—is an astonishing survivor among Paris's medieval architecture. It was commissioned by King Louis IX in the mid-13th century to house holy relics (such as the crown of thorns and pieces of the True Cross) that he had collected during the Crusades. (The relics are now kept in the treasury at Notre-Dame; see p. 49.) Along with the Conciergerie, the church is all that remains of the old Palais de la Cité, a former royal palace. The design is a mixture of flying buttresses, sumptuous woodwork, and dazzling ceilings. Original 13th-century stained-glass windows with 1,100 intricate biblical scenes transform the upper chapel into a translucent jewelry box. Ste.-Chapelle is enclosed within the **Palais de Justice,** a complex of 19th-century buildings that house the city's highest law courts.

4 blvd. du Palais, 1st arr. • tel 01 53 40 60 80 • Closed Jan. 1, May 1, and Dec. 25; Apr.–Dec. open until 7 p.m. • €€ • Métro: Cité, Châtelet, or St.-Michel • sainte-chapelle.fr

Place Louis Lépine

5 Named for a former police chief, this small square offers a splash of color amid the dour civic buildings that dominate the island's core. Tuesday through Saturday, an aromatic **flower market** takes over the space, dispensing a wide range of blooms, seeds, bulbs, and other gardening supplies. On Sundays, the square morphs into the **Marché aux Oiseaux** (Bird Market), where a wide variety of colorful birds and birdcages are sold.

Place Louis Lépine, 4th arr. • Métro: Cité

GOOD **EATS**

■ **AU VIEUX PARIS D'ARCOLE**
Steps away from Notre-Dame, this romantic inn offers hearty cuisine from the Aveyron region. **24 rue Chanoinesse, 4th arr., tel 01 40 51 78 52, closed Mon., €€–€€€**

■ **LE FLORE EN L'ÎLE**
Delicious desserts and drinks, and dreamy views of Notre-Dame, make this riverside café the sort of place you can linger for hours. **42 quai d'Orléans, 4th arr., tel 01 43 29 88 27, €–€€**

■ **NOS ANCÊTRES LES GAULOIS**
The hearty, fixed-price menu at this Île St.-Louis favorite runs heavy on crudités, grilled meats, and all the wine you can drink. **39 rue St.-Louis-en-l'Île, 4th arr., tel 01 46 33 66 07, €–€€**

Cathédrale de Notre-Dame de Paris

6 See pp. 48–49.

6 parvis de Notre-Dame, 4th arr. • tel 01 42 34 56 10 • Closed until further notice • Métro: Cité or St.-Michel • notredamedeparis.fr

Ancien Cloître Quartier

7 The warren of narrow lanes on the north side of Notre-Dame recalls the medieval urban landscape that once covered much of central Paris. Streets in the Ancient Cloister Quarter, such as **rue des Ursins** and **rue de la Colombe,** evoke a time when monks lived in the shadow of the great cathedral. **Rue Chanoinesse** is flanked by ancient clergymen's houses, as well as a newer building on the site of the dwelling *(No. 10)* where the tragic 12th-century love affair between Abélard and Héloïse allegedly played out.

Rue d'Arcole, 4th arr. • Métro: Cité or St.-Michel

Île St.-Louis

8 The petite Île St.-Louis floats beneath the radar of most visitors, a slice of the Parisian past that has somehow persevered. Originally used for grazing cattle, the marshy island was transformed in the 17th century into an aristocratic enclave, where many of the bright sparks of the Enlightenment lived, worked, or played. Although now heavily restored, most of the buildings date from that period, such as the **Hôtel de Lauzun** (*17 quai d'Anjou),* built in 1657, which was home

Historic town houses line rue St.-Louis en l'Île.

to the poets Charles Baudelaire (1811–67) and Théophile Gautier (1811–72), and the composer Richard Wagner (1813–83). The unstable land means many of the old buildings have subsided, or lean to the left or to the right. The island's only church, **St.-Louis-en-l'Île** (*19 rue St.-Louis en l'Île, 4th arr., tel 01 46 34 11 60, Mon. 6 p.m.–6:45 p.m. only, Tue.–Sun. closed 1–3 p.m.*) has several claims to fame, including an offbeat three-aisle configuration and an outdoor iron clock. Crowned by a narrow steeple that towers over the neighborhood, the baroque structure took more than a century (1656–1765) to complete. It is notable for its soaring Corinthian columns and grand organ, and as a venue for concerts of sacred music. Nowadays, Parisians flock to the island not so much for rich history as for the fruity ice cream scooped at **Berthillon** (*29–31 rue St.-Louis en l'Île*).

Pont de Sully, 4th arr. • Métro: Pont Marie

Cathédrale de Notre-Dame de Paris

Rising above the Île de la Cité, the cathedral of Notre-Dame is an example of medieval architectural genius.

Decapitated by the Romans, St. Denis is depicted holding his head in the cathedral's left portal.

"And the cathedral was not only company for him, it was the universe; nay, more, it was nature itself," wrote French writer Victor Hugo in *The Hunchback of Notre-Dame.* Hugo was speaking of the fictional Quasimodo, but he might as well have been referring to all mankind and its reaction to the Parisian church, built between 1163 and 1345. Few buildings have a more fabled story than this cathedral, whose history blends fact and fiction, making Notre-Dame both an architectural landmark and a cultural icon.

■ THE FACADE

Looming over Place de Parvis Notre-Dame, the cathedral facade is one of the great works of Gothic artistry. The **rose window** takes pride of place in the center—notice how it forms a massive halo around the Virgin and Child sculpture group—but your eye is also drawn to the massive portals that frame the three entrances. The **Portal of the Last Judgment,** which metaphorically opens the doors to the paradise within the cathedral, is flanked by the **Portal of the Virgin** (left) and the **Portal of St. Anne** (right). Running across the top of all three portals is the spectacular **King's Gallery,** with 28 statues of the ancient monarchs of Israel and Judea.

■ NAVE & CHANCEL

Even by today's standards, the cathedral's proportions are immense: The core is 427 feet long (130 m) and 115 feet high (35 m), flanked by 37 chapels and 75 giant stone pillars. Upwards of 9,000 people can worship within these hallowed walls. The massive rose windows and their glass bays are as tall as a six-story building.

AFTER **THE FIRE**

Notre-Dame is closed to the public until further notice. The fire in April 2019 destroyed the spire and two thirds of the roof, as well as damaging the side walls. Damage to the interior was limited.

The south window, installed in 1260, was a gift from St. Louis.

■ THE TOWERS

Realm of Victor Hugo's fictional bell-ringer Quasimodo, the cathedral's twin towers rise 226 feet (69 m) into the Parisian sky. The **Chimera Gallery,** about two-thirds of the way up, is the place to get up close and personal with Notre-Dame's gargoyles. But the best views are from the South Tower's roof.

■ THE TREASURY

Sacred objects from the birth of Christianity through modern times are safeguarded in the cathedral's treasury. Among the more noteworthy items are a golden shrine for the **Crown of Thorns,** as well as a **wooden fragment and nail,** presumed to be from the cross on which Jesus was crucified.

6 parvis de Notre-Dame, 4th arr. • tel 01 42 34 56 10 • Closed until further notice • Métro: Cité or St.-Michel • notredamedeparis.fr

Gothic Architecture

It may be hard to believe, but people once considered the Gothic architecture that we admire today to be ugly and retrograde. Renaissance pundits coined the term when trying to link a mode they considered lowbrow to the barbarian tribes that overran the Roman Empire. The Goths had nothing to do with the design that bears their name. It wasn't until the 19th century that Gothic architecture was seen as one of the great achievements of Western civilization.

The flying buttresses of Notre-Dame (above) can best be viewed from Square Jean XXIII, behind the cathedral. Ste.-Chapelle has one of the world's largest collections of stained glass (right).

Religious Powerhouses

The construction of St.-Denis (see p. 52) and Notre-Dame (see pp. 48–49) heralded the development of Gothic architecture in Paris in the early 12th century, when France had grown into a great power with an urge to express itself in grandiose buildings. This segued nicely with the Catholic Church's desire to create great temples to God, whereas the Romanesque style that had dominated from the ninth century limited height and decoration.

Building Tall

French architects and masons solved these engineering dilemmas with innovations that began around 1120—soaring arches, ribbed vaulting, and flying buttresses—the structural elements of Gothic architecture. Together these allowed for much taller structures, thinner walls, and larger windows, resulting in dazzling spaces filled with light. Add a touch of melodrama with gargoyles (waterspouts) and you have a startling new architectural form that swept across Europe.

Gothic Masterpeices

The **Basilique St.-Denis** in what is now suburban Paris, became the first true Gothic building thanks to a 12th-century renovation that added many of the new structural and design elements to the original eighth-century building. The nave and ambulatory became prototypes for similar creations.

Notre-Dame soon followed, with construction work starting about two decades after St.-Denis's renovation. The first of Europe's great Gothic cathedrals, everything about Notre-Dame was designed to impress, inspire, and intimidate anyone who gazed upon her. Although smaller than the other two, the royal chapel of **Ste.-Chapelle** (see p. 45), built to house holy relics, is considered the apex of Gothic decoration in Paris.

GOTHIC **TERMS**

Flying buttress An arch that takes the weight of a vault or roof from the upper part of a wall to an outer support.

Gargoyle A waterspout projecting from a roof or parapet, often depicting a grotesque figure or creature.

Pointed arches These arches help support the roof's weight, allowing for thinner walls.

Rib vault A stone rib supporting a vaulted ceiling.

Rose window A circular window with ornamental tracery. The west rose window in Notre-Dame is 31 feet (9.4 m) in diameter.

THE ISLANDS

Underground Paris

From Edgar Allan Poe and Victor Hugo to Anne Rice and her celebrated vampires, underground Paris has provided rich pickings for popular literature. But the city's subterranean world also has its factual side—royal tombs and Roman ruins, rat-infested sewers and solemn memorials.

■ BENEATH NOTRE-DAME

Notre-Dame's **Crypte Archéologique** (*7 parvis de Notre-Dame, 4th arr., tel 01 55 42 50 10, closed until further notice, crypte.paris.fr*) contains the remnants of various structures that have stood on this spot over the last 2,000 years, including a Gallo-Roman house, medieval shops, and a fourth-century bathhouse. Directly behind Notre-Dame, the subterranean **Mémorial des Martyrs de la Déportation** (*square de l'Île de France, 4th arr., tel 01 46 33 87 56, closed Mon.*) is dedicated to the 200,000 French who perished in Nazi concentration camps during World War II. Opened in 1962, the striking design is intended to evoke feelings of doom and claustrophobia.

■ OTHER CHURCH CRYPTS

The city's churches have their own sunken charms. The **Panthéon** (*place du Panthéon, 5th arr., tel 01 44 32 18 00, closed Jan. 1, May 1, and Dec. 25,* €€, *free on the first Sun. of the month*) crypt is the last resting place for many a famous Parisian, including Victor Hugo, Marie Curie, Émile Zola, Jean-Jacques Rousseau, and Voltaire. The crypt beneath the **Basilique St.-Denis** (*1 place de la Légion d'Honneur, 7th arr., tel 01 48 09 83 54, closed Jan. 1, May 1, and Dec. 25,* €€) is said to contain the remains of King Louis XVI and Queen Marie-Antoinette, as well as an ossuary holding the bones exhumed from royal tombs during the French Revolution.

■ SKULLS & GRAFFITI

Hundreds of abandoned mine shafts lie beneath Paris's streets, forming an underground labyrinth that has been used by secret societies, resistance movements, and raucous party animals for hundreds of years. Today, although most of these tunnels are strictly off-limits, a committed group of "cataphiles" defy the police to roam

THE ISLANDS

The remains of around six million Parisians make the city's catacombs an unusual attraction.

the network and express themselves away from society's glare. For visitors, the only accessible part of the network are the **Catacombes de Paris** (*1 ave. du Colonel Henri Roi-Tanguy, 14th arr., tel 01 43 22 47 63, closed Mon., Jan. 1, May 1, and Dec. 25, €€€, catacombes. paris.fr*), created in the late 18th century when authorities decided to relocate all of the city's medieval cemeteries— and their thousands of corpses—to the abandoned quarries. Victims of the revolution were among the first new bodies to be buried here. The subterranean trail leads past walls of human skulls and unusual graffiti.

Self-guided tours commence from Place Denfert-Rochereau on the Left Bank. The catacombs are temporarily closed from time to time, so check the website before your visit.

■ A Stroll in the Sewers
Another underground attraction is the sprawling **Musée des Égouts** ("Sewers Museum"; *pont de l'Alma, opposite 93 quai d'Orsay, 7th arr., tel 01 53 68 27 81; closed for renovation until early 2020*). Located in genuine sewage tunnels —with metal grates over the rushing water—the displays cover Paris sewers past, present, and future.

Quartier Latin

Although the name Latin Quarter (Quartier Latin) refers to the lingua franca of the scholars and teachers who began to congregate in this riverside neighborhood during medieval times, it is also a throwback to the area's first urbanizers. The Roman town of Lutetia (Lutèce) was founded on islands in the Seine, but it soon overflowed to the Left Bank. Here the Romans built a forum, public baths (Musée de Cluny), and an open-air arena (Arènes de Lutèce) where gladiators battled. By the Middle Ages, abbeys and monasteries dominated the area, creating a cluster of scholarship and learning that by the 13th century had evolved into a university called the Sorbonne. The French Revolution gutted many of the quarter's religious buildings, but the immense Panthéon was spared, transformed into an eternal tribute to the French giants of science, literature, and philosophy. Reflecting the ever-changing character of Paris, the area has also become a hub for the city's Muslim residents, home to France's largest mosque, and a thriving Arab art and culture center.

❶ **An eclectic mix of cafés, bars, and artisanal food stores line the crooked, close-packed streets of the Quartier Latin.**

Quartier Latin

Encounter Roman ruins, botanical gardens, and 21st-century riverfront architecture on a stroll in the Latin Quarter.

QUARTIER LATIN

❶ **St.-Séverin** (see p. 58) Gothic also comes in small packages, epitomized by the petite flamboyance of a church dedicated to a sixth-century hermit saint. Turn left out of the church, cross boulevard St.-Germain, and hang a quick right on rue Cluny.

❷ **Musée de Cluny** (see pp. 64–65) See Roman baths and a medieval mansion filled with artifacts from the Middle Ages in one of the city's best small museums. Cross the square in front of the museum, and follow rue de la Sorbonne along the west side of the university.

❸ **La Sorbonne** (see pp. 58–59) Many have found education and enlightenment within the walls of this hallowed university, founded in the 13th century as a theological college. Turn left on rue Cujas and continue to Place du Panthéon.

❹ **Panthéon** (see p. 59) This towering neoclassical church was converted during the revolution into a secular resting place for those who inspired France to greatness. Move one block east along Place du Panthéon.

❺ **St.-Étienne-du-Mont** (see p. 60) An elaborate rood screen dominates the nave of this simple yet sumptuous Gothic church. Walk two blocks east along rue Clovis, veer left on rue du Cardinal Lemoine and then right on rue Monge.

**QUARTIER LATIN   DISTANCE: 4 MILES (6.4 KM)
TIME: APPROX. 6–8 HOURS   MÉTRO START: ST.-MICHEL**

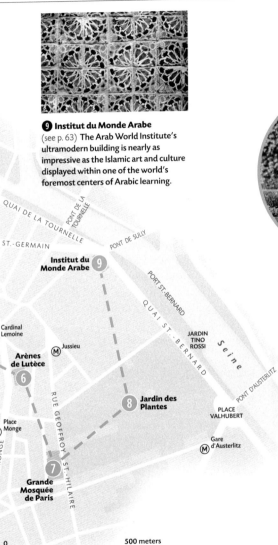

9 Institut du Monde Arabe
(see p. 63) The Arab World Institute's ultramodern building is nearly as impressive as the Islamic art and culture displayed within one of the world's foremost centers of Arabic learning.

8 Jardin des Plantes (see pp. 62–63) The city's botanical gardens blend flora, fauna, and museums. Exit the gardens via the Place Valhubert gate, and turn left on Quai St.-Bernard.

7 Grande Mosquée de Paris (see pp. 61–62) The mosque is a dazzling display of North African architecture. Cross rue Geoffroy St.-Hilaire to the gardens across the road.

6 Arènes de Lutèce (see pp. 60–61) Gladiatorial combat once took center stage at this ancient Roman arena, now a quiet park. On leaving, turn left on rue Lacépède and then right on rue Geoffroy St.-Hilaire.

St.-Séverin

1 Despite its diminutive size, the Latin Quarter's parish church embraces a long and incredibly rich history. Its patron saint was a sixth-century hermit monk who lived in Paris around the time that King Clovis decided to convert to Christianity and, in so doing, forever changed the fortunes of both the city and France. Construction of the current church was a protracted affair that commenced in the 13th century with the facade and nave, and ended in the 17th century when the cousin of King Louis XIV (Mademoiselle de Montpensier) hired royal architect Charles Le Brun to "modernize" the interior. He was careful to preserve the church's Flamboyant Gothic spirit, manifested in its copious **stained glass,** menacing **gargoyles,** and a **double ambulatory** lined with pillars that bear an uncanny resemblance to palm trees. St.-Séverin's steeple shelters the oldest **bell** in Paris (1412). The courtyard on the south side was once the parish burial ground; the cloister-like structure along the outer side is the city's only remaining charnel house. The church often hosts Saturday night **concerts.**

3 rue des Prêtres St.-Séverin, 5th arr. • tel 01 42 34 93 50 • Métro: Cluny – La Sorbonne or St.-Michel • saint-severin.com

One of a series of stained-glass windows by Jean-René Bazaine, installed between 1964 and 1969 in the church of St.-Séverin.

Musée de Cluny

2 See pp. 64–65.

6 place Paul Painlevé, 5th arr. • tel 01 53 73 78 00 • Closed Tues., Jan. 1, May 1, and Dec. 25 • € • Métro: Cluny – La Sorbonne, Odéon or St.-Michel • musee-moyenage.fr

La Sorbonne

3 One of the world's oldest and most prestigious institutes of learning, the Sorbonne traces its origins to the mid-13th century, when canon Robert de Sorbon (confessor to King Louis IX) created a theological college for poor students. From those humble beginnings rose today's campus, where more than 23,000 students and 1,300 teachers labor in 17 departments. Cardinal Richelieu oversaw construction of the present building during his tenure as the university's chancellor in the early 17th century. The main building is a maze of lecture halls and laboratories, **libraries** and offices, an **observatory,** and a Jesuit-style **church** where Richelieu is buried.

1 rue Victor Cousin, 5th arr. • tel 01 40 46 22 11 • Group tours only: minimum ten people, reservation required • €€ • Métro: Cluny – La Sorbonne • sorbonne.fr

Panthéon

4 Many French movers and shakers found their last resting spot inside this soaring Latin Quarter edifice. Although erected as a church dedicated to St. Genevieve, the massive structure was secularized during the revolution and transformed into a temple to fame where influential Frenchmen were buried. Among those interred within the **crypt** are philosophers Voltaire, Descartes, and Rousseau, writers Victor Hugo, Émile Zola, and Alexandre Dumas, inventor Louis Braille, and Nobel Prize-winning scientist Marie Curie (one of only two women buried there). Built from 1758 to 1789, the Panthéon was an early example of neoclassical architecture, with a facade modeled on the original Pantheon in Rome and a cavernous interior in the shape of a Greek cross. The ellipsoidal dome influenced the design of the U.S. Capitol Building.

Place du Panthéon, 5th arr. • tel 01 44 32 18 00 • Closed Jan. 1, May 1, and Dec. 25 • €€ • Métro: Cardinal Lemoine • paris-pantheon.fr

GOOD **EATS**

■ **L'ATELIER MAÎTRE ALBERT**
An informal outpost of celebrity chef Guy Savoy, this modern restaurant focuses on rôtisserie meats. Try crispy roasted chicken with buttery mashed potatoes. **1 rue Maître Albert, 5th arr., tel 01 85 15 22 87, €€–€€€**

■ **RESTAURANT LE ZIRYAB**
This airy rooftop restaurant at the Institut du Monde Arabe serves up fabulous Lebanese cuisine with dreamy views down the Seine to Notre-Dame. **1 rue des Fossés St.-Bernard, 5th arr., tel 01 40 51 34 76, €€€**

■ **LE REMINET**
Close to Shakespeare and Company, this cozy bistro has one of the best lunch deals in town, made using fresh, locally sourced ingredients. **3 rue des Grands Degrés, 5th arr., tel 01 44 07 04 24, €–€€€**

QUARTIER LATIN

St.-Étienne-du-Mont

5 Literally within the shadow of the much larger Panthéon, St.-Étienne, one of the many beautiful churches on the Left Bank, is often overlooked. However, it contains one item unique in Paris: an elegant stone **rood screen** across the middle of the nave. A common feature in Gothic churches, the rood screen separated the chancel or high altar from the congregation and provided an extra surface on which to hang Christian imagery or a large rood (crucifix). Most were demolished during the Counter-Reformation, but St.-Étienne's rood screen survived into the modern era. Like so many of the city's churches, this one is a hybrid of styles, one of the last Gothic churches erected in Paris and one of the first with Renaissance influence. Although it is hard to see amidst the urbanization, the church crowns a hill *(mont)* named for Paris patron St. Genevieve and once adjoined a great abbey also dedicated to her memory. The abbey (along with St. Genevieve's tomb) was destroyed during the anti-religious fervor that accompanied the revolution. Her **sarcophagus stone,** containing several relics, now rests inside St.-Étienne. The celebrated French playwright Jean Racine and the mathematician/philosopher Blaise Pascal are both buried here. The church's 17th-century organ is the focus of a year-round Saturday night concert series.

1 place Ste.-Geneviève, 5th arr. • tel 01 43 54 11 79 • Métro: Cardinal Lemoine • saintetiennedumont.fr

IN **THE KNOW**

A pastiche of Parisian life, **rue Mouffetard** traces the route of a Roman road through the Latin Quarter. First and foremost it is an outdoor food market where you can pick up all the ingredients you need for a picnic in the Jardin du Luxembourg or Jardin des Plantes (Botanical Gardens). "La Mouff" also attracts street performers, as well as those who relish moody neighborhood bars like **Requin Chagrin** (No. 10) and **Le Verre à Pied** (No. 118). Ernest Hemingway lived and wrote much of A Moveable Feast at **74 rue du Cardinal Lemoine,** just off Mouffetard.

Arènes de Lutèce

6 Nowadays, on a spot where gladiators once waged mortal combat, elderly men play *pétanque* (boules) among the remains of a Roman arena near the Jardin des Plantes (Botanical Gardens, see p. 62). Badly damaged when barbarians sacked Paris

The Grande Mosquée's tranquil garden is a good place to escape the area's busy streets.

in the late third century, the arena lay buried and forgotten for nearly 1,500 years until its accidental discovery in 1869. Since then, the open-air stadium has been partially excavated and reconstructed. Estimates put its bygone capacity at 10,000 to 17,000 spectators, who crowded into the stone bleachers to watch sporting events, circus acts, and theater productions. Among the ruins are barred **animal cages** and a **stone stage** with acoustical niches used to amplify dialogue during plays or speeches.

47 rue Monge, 5th arr. • Métro: Cardinal Lemoine, Jussieu, or Place Monge

Grande Mosquée de Paris

7 The Grand Mosque comes as something of a visual shock after the Gothic architecture that dominates so much of the quarter. The elegant Mudejar design permeates the complex, from the horseshoe arches and decorative tiles to the peaceful patios of the **garden**—which anyone can visit—the octagonal dome, and a 108-foot (33 m) minaret that towers above the neighborhood. France's largest place of Islamic worship was created in the early 1920s to express the nation's thanks to the hundreds of thousands of Muslims from the colonies who fought (and often died) alongside French troops in World War I. The materials and decorations—Lebanese cedar, North African copper, Persian carpets—were sourced throughout the Muslim world. During World War II, the mosque's mufti is credited with saving scores of local Jews from deportation to the Nazi death camps by giving them Muslim identification documents. The mosque's **hammam** (Turkish bath; *39 rue St.-Hilaire, tel 01 43 31 38 20, Tues. and Sun., men only; Mon., Wed., Thurs., and Sat., women only*) is open to the public regardless of faith. The complex has a small **souk** (market) offering North African crafts and a **restaurant** serving Middle Eastern cuisine. Enjoy a glass of authentic Moroccan mint tea on the covered terrace.

2 bis, place du Puits de l'Ermite, 5th arr. • tel 01 45 35 78 17 • Closed to visitors Fri. and Muslim holidays • € • Métro: Place Monge, Censier – Daubenton, or Jussieu • mosqueedeparis.net

Jardin des Plantes

8 This diverse green space on the eastern edge of the Latin Quarter does double duty as a crowd pleaser and serious research institute. The 69 acres (28 ha) of the Jardin des Plantes (Botanical Gardens) has enough to keep visitors busy for hours, especially those with smaller children. The **Ménagerie** is one of the world's oldest zoos, begun during the revolution with animals confiscated from the royal collection at Versailles. It is home to more than 1,000 animals, including rare red pandas and clouded leopards. The garden is also home to the **Musée National d'Histoire Naturelle**. Don't

The romantic Rose Garden in the Jardin des Plantes blooms to perfection in May and June.

miss the long procession of life-size stuffed animals crossing a recreation of the African savanna in the museum's **Grande Galerie de l'Évolution** (Evolution Gallery) or the skeletons of huge dinosaurs and birds in the **Galerie de Paléontologie** (Palaeontology Gallery). Plant-lovers will enjoy the gardens' world-class botanical collection, especially the **Alpine Garden**'s 2,000 or more species from the Alps, Pyrenees, and Himalaya, and the **Rose Garden**'s 170 varieties. The newly renovated glass-and-steel **Grandes Serres** (greenhouses) include a display of tropical plants from New Caledonia. And make sure you find your way to the gazebo at the center of the hilly, yew-hedged **maze** for some great views over Paris.

Entrances on rue Geoffroy St.-Hilaire, rue Cuvier, and Quai St.-Bernard, 5th arr. • tel 01 40 79 56 01 • Museums closed Tues., Jan. 1, May 1, and Dec. 25 • Zoo and museums: €€–€€€ • Métro: Gare d'Austerlitz, Censier – Daubenton, or Jussieu • jardindesplantesdeparis.fr

Institut du Monde Arabe

9 A striking contrast to the traditional design of the Grande Mosquée (see pp. 61–62), the Institut du Monde Arabe (Arab World Institute) is an unapologetically modern structure erected in the 1980s as a center for Arab and Islamic culture and studies. The southern facade of architect Jean Nouvel's masterpiece is clad in a massive **glass-and-metal screen** with geometric motifs that function as light-sensitive apertures, controlling how much sunlight penetrates into the building. The institute contains a library, an auditorium where music, dance, and theater are performed, and three floors of **museum** space showing artifacts both modern and ancient from around the Arab world. Taking pride of place on the top (ninth) floor is a Lebanese restaurant (see Good Eats, p. 59) and a **terrace** with fantastic views.

1 rue des Fossés St.-Bernard, 5th arr. • tel 01 40 51 38 38 • Closed Mon. • Museum: €€ • Métro: Jussieu or Cardinal Lemoine • imarabe.org

SAVVY **TRAVELER**

Slightly upstream from the Institut du Monde Arabe (Arab World Institute), on the Quai St.-Bernard, is **Jardin Tino Rossi**. This waterfront sculpture garden features works by international artists. On summer evenings, the space hosts free open-air dance lessons ranging from salsa and tango to hip-hop.

QUARTIER LATIN

Musée de Cluny

*This architectural complex blends Gothic town house,
Roman baths, and whimsical medieval garden.*

"The Promenade," a 500-year-old *mille fleurs* ("thousand flowers") tapestry

Officially it is called the Musée National du Moyen Âge (National Museum
of the Middle Ages), but Parisians are much more likely to use a simpler
appellation—Musée de Cluny. This Left Bank compound was owned by the avid
art collector and amateur archaeologist Alexandre du Sommerard in the early
19th century. On his death in 1842, the state purchased his house and collection
and turned them into an outstanding museum of medieval art, including
tapestries, sculptures, stained glass, gold and ivory objects, and furniture.

■ THE TOWN HOUSE

Although they were based at Cluny in eastern France, the politically astute abbots kept a Parisian residence in the 14th century to be close to the royal court and the nearby university. The current structure, dubbed the Hôtel de Cluny, is largely the work of the late 15th-century abbot Jacques d'Amboise. The meticulously restored manse features decorative turrets, crenellated walls, and steeply pitched roofs with dormers. It is an outstanding example of Gothic architecture, in particular the **chapel** and its French Flamboyant style vaulting (Room 20). The town house and the court are closed for renovation until the spring of 2021.

■ ROMAN BATHS

The bathhouse forming part of the ground floor was developed between the first and third centuries A.D., when Paris was a thriving Gallo-Roman town. Given the maritime motifs, it was probably constructed by the guild of Paris boatmen, and it is believed it was later destroyed by invading barbarians. The *frigidarium* (cold water bath; Room 9) houses artifacts from antiquity—seek out the **Sailors' Pillar** and the fragment

of a mosaic, **"Love Riding a Dolphin."** Remains of a *tepidarium, caldarium,* and gymnasium are also visible.

■ MEDIEVAL TREASURES

The museum's forte is the decorative arts of the Middle Ages and especially its rich collection of tapestries. One highlight among the works is **"The Lady and the Unicorn"** series of six tapestries displayed beneath the central rotunda (Room 13). They were woven in the Netherlands between 1484 and 1500 using wool and silk threads. Five of them each depict one of the senses; the sixth alludes to sensuality and bears the inscription "To my only desire."

DON'T **MISS**

The gardens of the Hôtel de Cluny have changed many times since first planted in the 15th century, most recently in 2000, when they were reworked along whimsical medieval lines. The **Unicorn Forest** was inspired by the celebrated tapestries, and a **kitchen garden** is stocked with herbs and vegetables that would have been popular in the Middle Ages. The **flower meadow** takes its cue from the museum's *mille fleurs* ("thousand flowers") tapestries.

6 place Paul Painlevé, 5th arr. • tel 01 53 73 78 00 • Closed Tues., Jan. 1, May 1, and Dec. 25 • € • Métro: Cluny – La Sorbonne, Odéon or St.-Michel • musee-moyenage.fr

Existentialists & Intellectuals

The Left Bank is famous as a haunt of disaffected intellectuals, aspiring writers, and bohemian artists. This reputation was mostly earned between the 1920s and the 1950s, from the era of America's "Lost Generation" to the high tide of French existentialism. Attracted by the freedom of expression that prevailed in Paris, writers from France and abroad colonized the bars, cafés, and salons and drew inspiration from their adopted city.

Philosopher, feminist theorist, and writer Simone de Beauvoir (above); Shakespeare and Company (right), a magnet for booklovers.

Writers' Enclave

American, British, and Irish writers flocked to Paris in the 1920s, including Ezra Pound, James Joyce, Ernest Hemingway, F. Scott Fitzgerald, Jean Rhys, Henry Miller, and George Orwell. They were drawn by the freedom and mental stimulation the city offered. Banned in their home countries, books such as Joyce's scatological masterpiece *Ulysses* (1922) and Miller's sexually explicit *Tropic of Cancer* (1934) could be printed and read in Paris.

Montparnasse Café Life

Support for aspiring writers was provided by American expatriates such as Sylvia Beach (see sidebar, opposite) and the fiercely modernist Gertrude Stein, who held a salon on rue de Fleurus, by the Jardin du Luxembourg. But the hub of intellectual life in this period lay in the cafés of Montparnasse, particularly **La Rotonde** *(105 blvd. du Montparnasse, 14th arr.)* and **Le Dôme** *(No. 108)*. Hemingway wrote most of *The Sun Also Rises* at a table in **La Closerie des Lilas** *(No. 171)*.

St.-Germain Celebrities

After the German occupation of 1940 to 1944, the focus of intellectual café life shifted northward to St.-Germain. At **Les Deux Magots** *(6 place St.-Germain-des-Prés, 6th arr.)* or **Café de Flore** *(172 blvd. St.-Germain, 6th arr.)*, the writers and philosophers Jean-Paul Sartre and Simone de Beauvoir held court as superstars of the trendsetting existentialist movement. In the postwar years they became the figureheads of a self-consciously disillusioned generation.

Today, the Left Bank cafés are still the natural habitat of many French intellectuals and writers, but they are considerably overwhelmed in numbers by the tourist hordes.

SHAKESPEARE
& COMPANY

American Sylvia Beach established the English-language bookshop Shakespeare and Company in 1919. Her premises at 12 rue de l'Odéon, 6th arr., were a haven for expatriate writers in the 1920s and 1930s. Beach's bookshop closed in 1941, but its name and tradition are maintained in the current Shakespeare and Company across the Pont au Double from Notre-Dame cathedral *(37 rue de la Bûcherie, 5th arr.).*

High-end Dining

Haute cuisine is alive and well in Paris, and visitors have a plethora of celebrated destinations to choose from. The chefs at these legendary restaurants have garnered 15 Michelin stars between them. A meal at one of their tables is not just lunch or dinner: it's an unforgettable experience.

QUARTIER LATIN

■ LA TOUR D'ARGENT

André Terrail took over this historic restaurant in the Latin Quarter, with its unrivaled view over the Seine and Notre-Dame, when his father Claude—a legend—died in 2006. He has injected the restaurant with new energy while maintaining many of its traditions, including the famous *canard Tour d'Argent* (pressed duck), *quenelles de brochet* (pike quenelles), and a superb wine list.

15 quai de la Tournelle, 5th arr., tel 01 43 54 23 31, €€€€€, tourdargent.com

■ L'ÉPICURE

Chef Éric Frechon has achieved the highly coveted award of three Michelin stars at Hôtel Le Bristol Paris just north of the Champs-Élysées. He dazzles diners with dishes like *homard bleu* (blue lobster with chestnuts) and *truffe noire du Périgord entiére* (whole black truffle from Périgord with Jerusalem artichoke). The light-filled dining room is the hotel's former summer terrace.

112 rue du Faubourg St.-Honoré, 8th arr., tel 01 53 43 43 40, €€€€€, oetkercollection.com

■ PIERRE GAGNAIRE

Chef Pierre Gagnaire has addresses around the world but still considers his eponymous restaurant north of the Champs-Élysées *le coeur*—the heart. The dining room is insulated from the outside world, elegant but subdued, with little to distract from the overwhelming series of inventive dishes that will cross your table, from the first amuse-bouche to the last sweet *mignardise*.

6 rue Balzac, 8th arr., tel 01 58 36 12 50, €€€€€, pierre-gagnaire.com

■ PAVILLON LEDOYEN

This regal, neoclassical pavilion near the Champs-Élysées is a temple of gastronomy. The first restaurant here appeared in 1779, when cows still

At L'Arpège, Alain Passard brings a delicate touch to the cooking of simple ingredients.

grazed the area. Since then, it has fed royalty, literati, and high society. Chef Yannick Alléno regales diners with classic French dishes with sauces that befit the luxe, romantic setting.

8 ave. Dutuit, 8th arr., tel 01 53 05 10 00, €€€€€, yannick-alleno.com

■ L'ARPÈGE

Alain Passard's sublime vegetables come direct from his own farm, but there's nothing rustic about a meal at L'Arpège, near Les Invalides. Yes, there are meat, fish, and fowl on the menu, but it's Passard's celebration of produce from the kitchen garden that has made him among the most influential chefs of the day.

84 rue de Varenne, 7th arr., tel 01 47 05 09 06, €€€€€, alain-passard.com

■ L'ASTRANCE

There's room for only 25 diners in this high-ceilinged, three-star restaurant near the Trocadéro—the theater for chef Pascal Barbot's imaginative, direct cooking. His signature galette of shaved raw *champignons de Paris* studded with *verjus*-marinated foie gras is a new classic.

4 rue Beethoven, 16th arr., tel 01 40 50 84 40, €€€€€, astrancerestaurant.com

St.-Germain & Montparnasse

An artistic flair still prevails in these two neighborhoods that stretch south from the Seine to the Cimetière du Montparnasse, whose tombstones commemorate the famous writers, artists, philosophers, and intellectuals who once frequented the area's cafés and gardens. Today, although the lively atmosphere of St.-Germain promises trendy shops and chic boutiques, you can still feel its creative history in the museums housing work by artists Eugène Delacroix and Ossip Zadkine. Enjoy a break from the hubbub with a stroll around the Jardin du Luxembourg, Paris's most popular park. The churches of St.-Germain-des-Prés and St.-Sulpice abound with interesting history and architecture. For a great view, head to the 56th floor of the Tour Montparnasse.

◀ **Les Deux Magots in the shadow of Église St.-Germain-des-Prés is a popular watering hole.**

St.-Germain & Montparnasse

Explore the parks and galleries of Paris's intellectual heart.

❶ Musée Delacroix (see p. 74) Romantic artist Eugène Delacroix's apartment and studio, along with his private garden, are tucked away in one of Paris's charming small squares. Walk south on rue de Furstemberg, then west on rue de l'Abbaye.

❷ Église St.-Germain-des-Prés (see p. 74) Once a sixth-century Benedictine abbey, Paris's oldest church has seen plenty of history. Walk south on rue Bonaparte.

❸ Église St.-Sulpice (see p. 75) Eugène Delacroix's murals decorate this large church, which also has one of the world's finest organs. Walk west on rue du Vieux Colombier, then turn south onto rue de Sèvres.

❹ La Grande Épicerie de Paris

Map labels:

Seine

PONT ROYAL
QUAI VOLTAIRE
QUAI MALAQUAIS
PONT DU CARROUSEL
QUAI DE CONTI
PONT DES ARTS
PONT NEUF
QUAI DES GRANDS AUGUSTINS

PONT ST.-MICHEL
PLACE ST.-MICHEL
Ⓜ St.-Michel
Cluny - La Sorbonne Ⓜ

RUE DES STS.-PÈRES

❶ Musée Delacroix

Église St.-Germain-des-Prés Ⓜ
St-Germain-des-Prés Ⓜ

Ⓜ Mabillon
BOULEVARD ST.-GERMAIN
Ⓜ Odéon

❷

BOULEVARD ST.-MICHEL

❸ Église St.-Sulpice
Ⓜ St.-Sulpice

PLACE ST.-SULPICE

RUE DE RENNES

BOULEVARD

PLACE LE CORBUSIER
Sèvres-Babylone Ⓜ

❹

RUE DE SÈVRES

Ⓜ Rennes

RASPAIL

Ⓜ St.-Placide

RUE DE RENNES

BD. DU
PLACE LÉON PAUL FARGUE
Ⓜ Duroc
RUE DE SÈVRES

Palais du Luxembourg

❺ Jardin du Luxembourg

PLACE EDMOND ROSTAND

0 — 500 meters
0 — 500 yards

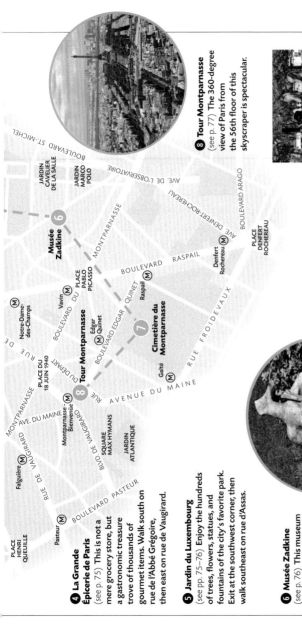

❽ Tour Montparnasse
(see p. 77) The 360-degree
view of Paris from
the 56th floor of this
skyscraper is spectacular.

**❼ Cimetière du
Montparnasse** (see
pp. 76–77) The final resting
place for writers, artists,
philosophers, musicians,
and actors. Exit the cemetery
at the northern entrance,
and walk west on boulevard
Edgar Quinet.

**❹ La Grande
Épicerie de Paris**
(see p. 75) This is not a
mere grocery store, but
a gastronomic treasure
trove of thousands of
gourmet items. Walk south on
rue de l'Abbé Grégoire,
then east on rue de Vaugirard.

❺ Jardin du Luxembourg
(see pp. 75–76) Enjoy the hundreds
of trees, flowers, statues, and
fountains of the city's favorite park.
Exit at the southwest corner, then
walk southeast on rue d'Assas.

❻ Musée Zadkine
(see p. 76) This museum
houses a collection of
work by Russian-born
sculptor and artist Ossip
Zadkine. Walk southwest
on rue Joseph Bara, turn
right and then left onto rue
de Chevreuse. Turn right onto
boulevard du Montparnasse and
then south on rue Huyghens.

**ST.-GERMAIN & MONTPARNASSE   DISTANCE: APPROX 3.1 MILES (5 KM)
TIME: APPROX. 6–7 HOURS   MÉTRO START: ST.-GERMAIN-DES-PRÉS**

ST.-GERMAIN & MONTPARNASSE

Musée Delacroix

1 The Romantic artist Eugène Delacroix moved here in 1857 to work at the nearby Église St.-Sulpice (see opposite), where he painted murals that cemented his reputation as one of France's foremost artists. The museum, which became a national site in 1971, includes the painter's apartment, studio, and private garden. The paintings, pastels, watercolors, drawings, and sketches on display, from the **"Magdalene in the Desert,"** one of his most acclaimed works, to the **"Self-Portrait as Ravenswood,"** one of his few paintings of himself, represent almost every phase of his creativity. Memorabilia including easels, art palettes, the artist's personal letters, and items from his Morocco trip are on display. You can also walk around his much loved garden.

6 rue de Furstemberg, 6th arr. • tel 01 44 41 86 50 • Closed Tues., Jan. 1, May 1, and Dec. 25; open until 9 p.m. on the first Tues. of the month • €€ • Métro: St.-Germain-des-Prés or Mabillon • musee-delacroix.fr

Église St.-Germain-des-Prés

2 Founded in 542 by King Childebert, Paris's oldest church was once part of a powerful and rich abbey. The current building, dating from the 11th century, retains some of its **sixth-century columns**—part of an interior that includes Gothic vaulting and Romanesque arches. The abbey closed during the French Revolution after a mob stormed its prison during the September Massacres, when many suspected counterrevolutionaries were killed. Gunpowder was later stored in the abbey, which exploded in 1794, destroying many of its buildings; the church was heavily restored in the 19th century. The dimly lit building holds the **tomb of René Descartes** (1596–1650), the father of modern philosophy.

3 place St.-Germain-des-Prés, 6th arr. • tel 01 55 42 81 18 • Métro: St.-Germain-des-Prés • eglise-saintgermaindespres.fr

GOOD **EATS**

■ **LE CAFÉ DE LA MAIRIE**
Close to St.-Sulpice, the café offers sandwiches and hot meals.
8 place St.-Sulpice, 6th arr., tel 01 43 26 67 82, €€

■ **LA CLOSERIE DES LILAS**
Legendary bistro where Picasso, Hemingway, and Jean-Paul Sartre used to dine. **171 blvd. du Montparnasse, 6th arr., tel 01 40 51 34 50, €€€**

■ **SEMILLA**
A bistro serving contemporary cuisine next to rue de Buci.
54 rue de Seine, 6th arr., tel 01 43 54 34 50, €€

Église St.-Sulpice

3 The building of Paris's second largest church (after Notre-Dame) began in 1646 and took more than a hundred years. Three glorious Eugène Delacroix murals—**"Jacob Wrestling an Angel," "St. Michael Killing the Dragon,"** and **"Heliodorus Driven from the Temple"**—adorn the chapel to the right of the door. The church also houses one of the city's largest **organs,** whose 6,588 pipes fill the air with music after Sunday Mass.

Place St.-Sulpice, 6th arr. • tel 01 46 33 21 78 • Métro: St. Sulpice

The church of St.-Sulpice was the site of French writer Victor Hugo's wedding.

La Grande Épicerie de Paris

4 Foodie or not, everyone will appreciate this mammoth store full of gourmet delights. Twenty bakers and 25 pastry chefs produce buttery croissants, 70 specialty breads, artistic éclairs, petit fours, and dozens of other pastries every morning. You'll also find hot and cold cuisine from around the world, 57 kinds of bottled water, dozens of olive oils, and hundreds of cheeses. Don't forget the **wine cellar** either.

38 rue de Sèvres, 7th arr. • tel 01 44 39 81 00 • Closed Jan. 1, Easter Mon., Aug. 15, and Dec. 25 • Métro: Sèvres–Babylone • lagrandeepicerie.fr

Jardin du Luxembourg

5 This 60-acre (2.4 ha) oasis of greenery adjacent to the Luxembourg Palace (home of the French Senate) is Paris's favorite park. Queen Marie de Médicis constructed the garden and palace in the early 17th century to replicate her childhood home in Florence. Today, elm trees, apple and pear orchards, and formal flower beds fill the park, along with more than a hundred statues, including a small study of the **Statue of Liberty.** The **Médicis Fountain** is one of

IN **THE KNOW**

Montparnasse (Mount Parnassus) takes its name from the mythical home of the Greek gods. Once the haunt of poetic students, the original hill was flattened in 1725. The area became known for cabarets and bohemian cafés that attracted struggling artists and writers such as Pablo Picasso, Marc Chagall, Ernest Hemingway, F. Scott Fitzgerald, and James Joyce.

the most beautiful water features in Paris. The park is a great place for kids, who enjoy sailing model boats on the octagonal pond. The play area includes pony rides, an old-fashioned puppet show, and even a classic merry-go-round.

Rue de Médicis – rue de Vaugirard, 6th arr. • tel 01 42 64 33 99 • Métro: Odéon • senat.fr/visite/jardin

Musée Zadkine

⑥ Around 300 sculptures from Russian-born 20th-century artist Ossip Zadkine are on display at his former cottage home. He gained an international reputation with his cubist-inspired and abstract sculpture, culminating in his famous "The Destroyed City," a memorial to the destruction of Rotterdam in World War II. You can see a miniature of this piece, **"Torso of the Ruined Town,"** in the cottage's pleasant garden, along with the rest of the museum's larger works. Gallery Two holds a selection of his cubist sculptures, such as **"Woman and Fan"** in bronze and **"Beautiful Servant Girl"** in stone. Gallery Four is dedicated to works in wood—a medium that Zadkine was particularly interested in—and includes sculpture from throughout his career. The museum also hosts exhibitions from guest artists.

100 bis rue d'Assas, 6th arr. • tel 01 55 42 77 20 • Closed Mon. and public holidays • Free; temporary exhibitions: €–€€ , free under 18 • Métro: Vavin • zadkine.paris.fr

Cimetière du Montparnasse

⑦ In 1824, three farms were combined to form what became one of Paris's most famous cemeteries. The 47-acre (19 ha) burial ground is the final resting place for more than 300,000 people, including many of the area's luminaries. Just inside the entrance, where you can pick up a free map, are the **joint plots** of the philosophers Jean-Paul Sartre and his companion Simone de

Fans still commemorate French singer Serge Gainsbourg at Cimetière du Montparnasse.

Beauvoir. Wander around the cemetery's garden-like setting, with wide, paved walkways, fountains, and sculptures, to stumble across **tombs** of well-known people, such as poet Charles Baudelaire, author Susan Sontag, and Irish playwright Samuel Beckett.

3 blvd. Edgar Quinet, 14th arr. • tel 01 44 10 86 50 • Métro: Edgar Quinet or Raspail

Tour Montparnasse

Towering 690 feet (210 m) above the ground, this often-criticized building opened in 1973 and dwarfs everything else in the district. The 56th floor remains the main attraction, with a spectacular 360-degree view that extends up to 40 miles (64 km) on a clear day. The floor has displays of the city's monuments, a 15-minute film, photo exhibits, a gift shop, bar, café, and a gourmet restaurant, **Le Ciel de Paris** *(tel 01 40 64 77 64, reservation only, €€–€€€€€)*.

33 ave. du Maine, 15th arr. • tel 01 45 38 52 56 • Elevator to 56th floor: €€€€ • Métro: Montparnasse–Bienvenüe • tourmontparnasse56.com

Parks & Gardens

Parisian gardens were a sign of riches and power for the royal, wealthy, and noble, who created idyllic landscapes as a backdrop for elaborate parties, entertainments, and theatrical events. Over the centuries, French gardens took many forms according to the fashions of the times. The formal garden, however, was the most influential and enduring style—it is what we think of as the quintessential French garden.

You can rent model sailboats (above) in several of Paris's gardens. The Jardin du Luxembourg (right) is a popular place to rest in the summer sun.

Royal Gardens

Italian Renaissance gardens, inspired by classical ideals of beauty and order, were a heavy influence on *jardins à la française.* Queen Catherine de Médicis, the Italian wife of King Henri II, built one of Paris's oldest gardens, the **Jardin des Tuileries** (see pp. 118–119), in 1564, in an Italian style. In the 17th-century, landscape designer André Le Nôtre redrew the garden in its present form. He was a master of French formal gardens and his geometric shapes and symmetrical patterns aimed to show man's control over nature, and thus the power and prestige of the garden's owner.

The **Jardin du Luxembourg** (see pp. 75–76) was created in 1612 by another Italian, Queen Marie de Médicis, to remind her of the gardens of her youth. In the 19th century, architect Jean-François-Thérèse Chalgrin restored the gardens, which are composed of several parts—a formal garden, an "English" garden, a woody area, lawns, and an orchard—all crossed by paths that beckon visitors to take a relaxing stroll.

Second Empire Legacy

Today's Parisian gardens owe their appearance to Second Empire fashion. After the French Revolution, formal gardens with their strict, symmetrical forms were discarded in favor of an English style that re-created an idyllic pastoral landscape, complete with lakes, bridges, ruins, and temples—such as **Parc Monceau** (see p. 136). At the same time, the creation of green space became necessary to provide the city's population with some fresh air. Nineteenth-century city planner Baron Haussmann created the **Bois de Boulogne** and the **Bois de Vincennes,** which were landscaped with open lawns and woodlands; these immense parks still constitute the city's largest green spaces.

MODERN **PARKS**

André Citroën Park
Opened in 1992, this park on the former site of the Citroën factory comprises a central lawn around fountains, greenhouses, a canal, and small gardens. **2 rue Cauchy, 15th arr., paris.fr/equipements/parc-andre-citroen-1791**

Fondation Louis Vuitton
Designed by Frank Gehry, this staggering new museum houses the private art collection of Bernaud Arnault, CEO of LVMH. Nicknamed "The Iceberg," the building has 12 architectural sails with 3,600 glass panels. **8 ave. du Mahatma Gandhi, Bois de Boulogne, fondationlouisvuitton.fr**

Small Museums

Paris may be renowned for colossal collections such as the Louvre, but the French capital also boasts an array of great small museums, including the homes of artists, writers, and singers, and a homage to wine.

■ MUSÉE BOURDELLE

Sculpture and other art fills the Montparnasse home, garden, and workshop of 19th-century artist Antoine Bourdelle—a protégé of Auguste Rodin. From its 21 dramatic **busts of Beethoven** to figures from Greek mythology and sensuous **female nudes,** the collection reflects Bourdelle's range. The museum also houses art from Rodin, Eugène Delacroix, and other artists.

18 rue Antoine Bourdelle, 15th arr. • tel 01 49 54 73 73 • Closed Mon. and public holidays • Free; temporary exhibitions: €€ , free under 18 • Métro: Montparnasse–Bienvenüe or Falguière • bourdelle.paris.fr

■ MAISON DE VICTOR HUGO

France's preeminent author of *Les Misérables* and *The Hunchback of Notre Dame,* Victor Hugo, wrote many of his works on the second floor of this former hotel in Le Marais, where he lived from 1832 to 1848. Reopening in March 2020 after renovation works, the reconstructed rooms display photos, furniture, documents, and other mementos from his life, including 450 of his sketches and drawings.

6 place des Vosges, 4th arr. • tel 01 42 72 10 16 • Closed Mon. and public holidays • Métro: Bastille or Saint Paul • maisonsvictorhugo.paris.fr

■ MUSÉE DE LA VIE ROMANTIQUE

The charming Museum of Romantic Life in Montmartre was the former home of Dutch-born painter Ary Scheffer, who lived here in the early-to-mid-1800s. Scheffer held Friday night salons, attended by neighborhood artists and writers, including George Sand, Frédéric Chopin, and Eugène Delacroix. Visit the main house and its two studios, then the café in its peaceful garden. Among the permanent exhibits is George Sand's jewelry collection. The museum also hosts temporary exhibits.

16 rue Chaptal, 9th arr. • tel 01 55 31 95 67 • Closed Mon. and public holidays • €€€€ • Métro: Saint-Georges, Pigalle, or Blanche • museevieromantique.paris.fr

The Great Hall at the Musée Bourdelle.

■ Musée du Vin

The medieval stone-walled cellars of a 15th-century monastery close to the Jardins du Trocadéro house the museum of the Conseil des Échansons de France, a group devoted to fine French wine. Displays, waxwork figures, and artifacts such as wine bottles, corkscrews, and decanters demonstrate viticulture techniques throughout the ages. There are a shop and a restaurant, and you can also enjoy a wine-tasting session delivered by an expert.

5 square Charles Dickens, 16th arr. • tel 01 45 25 63 26 • Closed Mon., Sun., and public holidays • €€€ • Métro: Passy • museeduvinparis.com

■ Musée Marmottan– Claude Monet

Art historian Paul Marmottan bequeathed his house on the edge of Bois de Boulogne, together with his extensive collection of Renaissance, Consular, and First Empire art, to the Institut de France in 1932. The collection was expanded in 1966, when Impressionist Claude Monet's son donated 65 of his father's works, including several **Water Lilies** and **"Impression–Sunrise"** from the Rouen Cathedral Series.

2 rue Louis Boilly, 16th arr. • tel 01 44 96 50 33 • Closed Mon., Jan. 1, May 1, and Dec. 25 • €€€ Métro: La Muette or Ranelagh • marmottan.fr

Châtelet & Les Halles

For more than 800 years, the neighborhood of Les Halles held Paris's central food market. Today, the area is dominated by the Forum des Halles shopping mall, and yet there are still enough butchers, small markets, and food shops in the side streets to feel like you're in "the belly of Paris" during its heyday. To the east, some of the city's oldest streets surround the modernistic Centre Pompidou—one of the world's leading venues for contemporary art. Head south and you'll come to the Hôtel de Ville, seat of the city government since the 14th century and once the site of Paris's main port. Place du Châtelet marks the location of a long-gone fortress that once guarded a gate into the city. The whole area contains a treasury of monuments.

❶ **Église St.-Eustache has served some notable parishioners, including Cardinal Richelieu, Mozart, and Madame de Pompadour.**

Châtelet & Les Halles

The area around Paris's former central market has one of the world's best museums of contemporary art and many historic squares and streets.

1 Église St.-Eustache (see p. 86) Start at the Church of St.-Eustache, an unfinished masterpiece of Gothic architecture. Head east on rue Rambuteau, and turn south on rue Pierre Lescot.

2 Forum des Halles & Jardin Nelson Mandela (see pp. 86–87) The former site of the central food market is a large public garden above an underground shopping mall.

3 Fontaine des Innocents (see p. 87) This beautiful nymph-adorned, Renaissance-style fountain sits in the Place Joachim du Bellay. Continue on rue Berger, cross boulevard de Sébastopol, and walk two blocks to Place Georges Pompidou.

4 Centre Pompidou (see pp. 90–91) This cultural center is home to the Musée National d'Art Moderne, and the building is an attraction in itself. Head east on rue Aubry le Boucher, turn right on rue du Renard, and left on rue de Rivoli, to reach Place de l'Hôtel de Ville.

CHÂTELET & LES HALLES DISTANCE: 1 MILE (1.6 KM)
TIME: APPROX. 4 HOURS MÉTRO START: LES HALLES

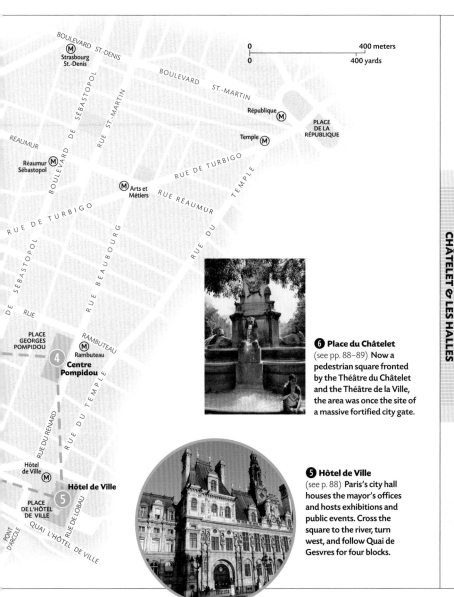

0 _____ 400 meters
0 _____ 400 yards

BOULEVARD ST-DENIS

Ⓜ Strasbourg St.-Denis

BOULEVARD ST.-MARTIN

RUE ST.-MARTIN

BOULEVARD DE SÉBASTOPOL

RÉAUMUR

Ⓜ Réaumur Sébastopol

République Ⓜ

Temple Ⓜ

PLACE DE LA RÉPUBLIQUE

RUE DE TURBIGO

Ⓜ Arts et Métiers

RUE RÉAUMUR

RUE DU TEMPLE

RUE DE TURBIGO

DE SÉBASTOPOL

RUE

RUE BEAUBOURG

PLACE GEORGES POMPIDOU

RAMBUTEAU

Ⓜ Rambuteau

④ Centre Pompidou

RUE DU TEMPLE

RUE DU RENARD

Hôtel de Ville Ⓜ

Hôtel de Ville

RUE DE LOBAU

PLACE DE L'HÔTEL DE VILLE

⑤

PONT D'ARCOLE

QUAI L'HÔTEL DE VILLE

❻ Place du Châtelet
(see pp. 88–89) Now a pedestrian square fronted by the Théâtre du Châtelet and the Théâtre de la Ville, the area was once the site of a massive fortified city gate.

❺ Hôtel de Ville
(see p. 88) Paris's city hall houses the mayor's offices and hosts exhibitions and public events. Cross the square to the river, turn west, and follow Quai de Gesvres for four blocks.

Église St.-Eustache

1 The first church to occupy this site was founded in 1223 by a local resident named Jean Alaias. Alaias had loaned King Philippe-Auguste a substantial sum; as repayment, the king authorized him to take a percentage from every bushel of fish sold at the neighboring market, and Alaias used his resulting fortune to build a chapel. Construction of the current church began in 1532 and took more than a hundred years. The structure is Gothic, with flying buttresses on the exterior and ribbed vaulting in the nave, but arches, columns, and pillars from the Renaissance fill the interior. Like many of Paris's churches, St.-Eustache was pillaged during the revolution and subsequently used as a barn. Now restored, its interior includes **stained-glass windows** created by Antoine Soulignac in 1632, several paintings by Peter Paul Rubens, including the **"Emmaus Pilgrims,"** and a modern sculpture by Raymond Mason, **"The Departure of Fruit and Vegetables from the Heart of Paris on the 28th February 1969,"** in one of the side chapels. The church has a strong musical tradition—Liszt and Berlioz performed here—and, with 8,000 pipes, the **Van den Heuvel organ** is among Paris's largest.

146 rue Rambuteau, 1st arr. • tel 01 42 36 31 05 • Métro: Châtelet or Étienne Marcel • saint-eustache.org

Forum des Halles & Jardin Nelson Mandela

2 Paris's central market stood in Les Halles from the 12th century to 1969. It began in the open, but in 1181, King Philippe-Auguste built two halls to shelter textile makers, and in 1543 King François I had additional buildings constructed in order to improve the market's hygiene. Sanitation problems continued to plague the area until the 1850s, when Napoleon III ordered improvements be made, including the construction of cast-iron-and-glass pavilions designed by architect Victor Baltard. In 1969, the market moved to Rungis, a southern suburb of Paris, and Baltard's pavilions were demolished. The only architectural remnant of the old market is the **Bourse du Commerce,** the rotunda at the western end of the gardens that once served as a grain market. The present **Forum des Halles**, built in 1979, is a subterranean shopping center topped by **public gardens**, which have been recently re-landscaped and refurbished with a large, modern playground. The shopping center itself has undergone a metamorphosis (completed in 2018) that embraces culture with an auditorium/recording studio, a conservatory, a media library, and a wider range of retail and culinary products. The epitome of this transformation is La Canopée, an enormous canopy of glass and metal that captures solar energy and serves as the entrance to the center.

101 rue Berger, 1st arr. • Métro: Châtelet • forumdeshalles.com

Fontaine des Innocents

Paris's only Renaissance fountain was built in 1549 to commemorate King Henri II's first entry into the city. Originally positioned against the wall of the Cimetière des Sts.-Innocents, on the corner of rue Berger and rue St.-Denis, notables used it as a viewing platform to watch Henri's procession.

This enormous fountain was designed by Palais du Louvre architect Pierre Lescot (see pp. 122–125) and decorated by sculptor Jean Goujon in the style of a Roman triumphal arch, with **relief carvings** of *putti* (cherubs) and veiled nymphs pouring water between Corinthian columns. In 1810, the bas-reliefs around the base were removed to the Louvre so they would not be eroded by the water flowing over them from the large brass font.

Place Joachim du Bellay, rue St.-Denis, 1st arr. • Métro: Châtelet

Centre Pompidou

See pp. 90–91.

Place Georges Pompidou, 4th arr. • tel 01 44 78 12 33 • Closed Tues. and May 1 • Musée National d'Art Moderne: €€€; access to Level 6 walkway: € • Métro: Rambuteau, Châtelet, or Hôtel de Ville • centrepompidou.fr

Water gushes down the stepped pedestal of the Fontaine des Innocents, decorated with cherubs and nymphs.

Hôtel de Ville

5 Paris's city hall has played a central role in civic life since the 11th century, as a center of commerce, government, public demonstrations, and no small number of executions. In 1264, under the auspices of King Louis IX, merchants elected the city's first municipal authority figures. In 1357, provost Étienne Marcel bought a mansion by the Seine to use for meetings, and since then the city government has been located on this spot. During the 1871 uprising the current building, dating from 1628, was consumed by fire. The hall's present appearance—ornately decorated with turrets and detailed stonework—dates from the heavy restoration that took place from 1874 to 1882. The facade is adorned with 30 statues representing French towns and 108 statues of famous people born in Paris. An allegorical figure representing Paris sits above the clock. Inside are the mayor's offices and exhibition spaces.

Until 1830, the **Place de l'Hôtel de Ville** was called the Place de Grève. *Grève* means "beach," or "strand," and traders and merchants used this spot as a riverside port to bring their goods into the city. The expression *faire la grève,* meaning "to go on strike," originated here, where unhappy workers gathered to protest. Today the square is used for concerts, festivals, and other events.

29 rue de Rivoli, 4th arr. • tel 01 42 76 40 40 • Group visits only; reservations required at: visites.hdv@paris.fr, • tel 01 42 76 54 04 • Métro: Hôtel de Ville • paris.fr/municipalite/l-hotel-de-ville

GOOD **EATS**

■ **LA RÉGALADE ST.-HONORÉ**
This second location of the classic La Régalade, near the Jardin Nelson Mandela, serves up seasonal bistro cooking from chef Bruno Doucet. **106 rue St.-Honoré, 1st arr., tel 01 42 21 92 40, €€€**

■ **CHAMPEAUX**
Chef Alain Ducasse's new-concept brasserie serves French dishes for every occasion in the shade of La Canopée. **Porte Rambuteau, 1st arr., tel 01 53 45 84 50, €–€€€**

■ **CHEZ DENISE**
The old food market lives on at this classic, meat-heavy restaurant to the east of the Forum des Halles. **5 rue des Prouvaires, 1st arr., tel 01 42 36 21 82, €€€**

CHÂTELET & LES HALLES

Place du Châtelet

6 This pedestrianized square is named for the Grand Châtelet, a 12th-century fortified city gate that protected the Île de la Cité and later housed courts, police offices, and a prison that was even

A temporary sculpture installation fills the Place de l'Hôtel de Ville.

more feared for its unpleasant conditions than the nearby Bastille. Napoleon destroyed the fort in 1808 and created the present-day square. At the center is the **Fontaine du Palmier** (Palmier Fountain), topped by a column erected in 1808 to honor Napoleon's victories in Egypt and Italy. Facing onto the square are two Haussmann-era theaters, **Théâtre de la Ville** *(2 place du Châtelet, 4th arr., tel 01 42 74 22 77, theatredelaville-paris.com; venue closed until Sept. 2021)* and **Théâtre du Châtelet** *(2 rue Edouard Colonne, 1st arr., tel 01 40 28 28 40, chatelet.com),* designed by architect Jean-Antoine-Gabriel Davioud and built in the early 1860s. The neighboring garden focuses on the **Tour St.-Jacques,** a Gothic tower from a church that was destroyed following the French Revolution. Pilgrims used the church, built by the butchers' guild, as a meeting point on their way to Santiago de Compostela in Spain.

Quai de la Mégisserie/blvd. de Sébastopol, 1st and 4th arr. • Métro: Châtelet

Centre Pompidou

The Centre Pompidou is a cultural institution showcasing modern and contemporary visual arts, music, performance, and film.

With so much on the outside (such as escalators), Centre Pompidou has more room for art.

Designed by architects Renzo Piano and Richard Rogers in 1977, the building housing the Centre Pompidou wears its inner workings—electricity, water, and air—on the outside in a primary-color maze of pipes and ducts. The popular Public Information Library occupies the first three levels, but the main attraction is the Musée National d'Art Moderne (the National Museum of Modern Art), a world-class collection of visual and multimedia works from 1905 to the present on Levels 4 and 5, plus changing exhibitions on Level 6.

■ MILESTONES IN MODERN ART

To visit the Musée National d'Art Moderne take the glass-enclosed escalator to the museum entrance on Level 5. With galleries arranged on two floors, the museum showcases the history of art from 1905 to the present day, and focuses on the most important art movements of the time—fauvism, cubism, and surrealism. The pieces on view are rotated once a year. Highlights on Level 5 include Picasso's **"Harlequin and Woman with a Necklace," "Portrait of the Journalist Sylvia von Harden,"** by Otto Dix, Francis Bacon's **"Three Figures in a Room,"** and several studies by Henri Matisse for a chapel he built in the French village of Vence.

■ CONTEMPORARY COLLECTION

A staircase leads down from Level 5 to Level 4, which exhibits art, architecture, and design from 1980 to present. Watch for Petrit Halilaj's sculpture entitled **"It is the first time dear that you have a human shape (spider),"** one of several pieces that the artist fashioned from metal structures and house ruins. The final room in the Contemporary Collection houses recent acquisitions of important multi-disciplinary

SAVVY **TRAVELER**

For €5, you can skip the museum and go straight to Level 6 for one of the best views of Paris.

artists such as Barnett Newman, Gil J. Wolman, and Vittorio Gregotti.

■ DINE ON SET

The chic restaurant **Georges** (tel 01 44 78 47 99, €€€–€€€€) on Level 6 is often likened to a Stanley Kubrick film set and serves an eclectic menu of French, American, and Asian cuisine. In spring and summer, dine on the outdoor terrace with sweeping views of the Paris skyline.

■ PLACE GEORGES POMPIDOU

The **Atelier Brancusi** is a time capsule of the sculptor Constantin Brancusi's studio, more or less as he left it when he died in 1957. Four sections of his studio have been re-created and include finished works as well as models, sketches, tools, and furniture. The square itself hosts outdoor art installations and some of Paris's best performance art and street theater.

Place Georges Pompidou, 4th arr. • tel 01 44 78 12 33 • Closed Tues. and May 1 • Musée National d'Art Moderne: €€€; access to Level 6 walkway: € • Métro: Rambuteau, Châtelet, or Hôtel de Ville • centrepompidou.fr

CHÂTELET & LES HALLES

Culinary Capital

The French love their food. Indeed, the restaurant, derived from the French word *restaurer* (to restore), is believed to have originated in Paris in 1765 with Monsieur Boulanger, who served a selection of pig's-and-sheep's-foot broths to workers in Les Halles. Soon establishments devoted entirely to eating were springing up all over the city, including Café de Chartres (renamed Le Grand Véfour; see p. 121), which has served fine food to the city's elite for more than 200 years.

CHÂTELET & LES HALLES

A chocolate and grapefruit dessert (above) at Le Grand Véfour (see p. 121); shoppers browse in E. Dehillerin (right), founded in 1820 and one of Paris's top specialist cookware shops.

Luxury Eateries

Monsieur Boulanger's success inspired many copies. Paris's first luxury restaurant, La Grande Taverne de Londres, opened in 1782. Its owner, former royal chef Antoine Beauvilliers, was the first to combine great food with excellent service, decor, and fine wine in a public eatery. By 1804, more than 500 restaurants served Parisians.

In the late 19th century, Auguste Escoffier introduced the *brigade de cuisine* system (influenced by his army days), which ran kitchens on a strictly hierarchical order from head chef to dishwasher— a system which is still in use today. Along with his partner, César Ritz, Escoffier opened the Hôtel Ritz, where his cooking earned him the title *Roi des Cuisiniers et Cuisinier des Rois* (King of Chefs and Chef of Kings).

Cordon Bleu

As access to fine dining increased, so did interest in cooking. In 1896, French journalist Marthe Distel founded *La Cuisinière Cordon*

Bleu culinary magazine. The name comes from a 16th-century order of knights, who wore *cordons bleus* (blue ribbons) to signify their status. To gain subscribers, Distel also offered cooking classes with some of Paris's top chefs, which soon developed into the world's first cooking school. The magazine and classes were a great success and helped to define French cuisine and spread its popularity throughout the world.

Michelin Status

In 1923, André Michelin added a star to the best restaurants in his drivers' guide book. Following World War II, the Michelin Guide spread across the world, cementing the French reputation as the experts on fine dining (See High-end Dining pp. 68–69).

PARIS **BISTROS**

The word "bistro" refers to smaller restaurants with a proprietor present—either in the kitchen or front of house—and typically serving simple food at reasonable prices, without ceremonious extras. The early 21st century saw the rise of the "neo-bistro," a movement initiated by young chefs who chose to forgo careers in Michelin-starred kitchens, instead choosing more relaxed settings to showcase their creativity and skills.

Street Markets & *Brocantes*

To experience Paris one must shop in Paris, especially at the famous *brocantes* (secondhand stalls) and *marchés aux puces* (antique flea markets). Despite its history, Les Halles is now known for its modern mall—but check out some of these markets and join your fellow Parisians as they root out a good buy.

CHÂTELET & LES HALLES

■ Raspail

Conventional stalls fill this St.-Germain street on Tuesday and Friday mornings, but on Sunday mornings it is one of the city's best *biologique* (organic) food markets. The roasted free-range chicken is delicious. Also look for unusual preserves.

Blvd. Raspail between rue du Cherche-Midi and rue de Rennes, 6th arr. • Open Tues., Fri., and Sun. a.m.

■ Marché aux Puces de la Porte de Vanves

South of Montparnasse, this market spread over two avenues offers antiques and bric-a-brac of all sorts and periods. Go early for bargains and the best pieces.

Ave. Georges Lafenestre and ave. Marc Sangnier, 14th arr. • Open Sat. and Sun. 7 a.m.–7:30 p.m.

■ Marché des Enfants Rouges

Named for the red-clothed children who lived at the former orphanage on this site, Paris's oldest covered market dates from the 1600s. It is more a fun place to have lunch or an early dinner in trendy Le Marais than it is a place to pick up great buys. The Japanese and Moroccan take-out stands are particularly good.

Rue de Bretagne, 3rd arr. • Closed Mon.

■ Marché Bastille

The Bastille area hosts the city's largest and most impressive market. Famed for its fresh food produce (the cheeses are excellent), the market is popular with Parisians because of the huge variety offered—everything from food to clothing to kitchen tools.

Blvd. Richard Lenoir between rue Amelot and rue St.-Sabin, 11th arr. • Open Thurs. 7 a.m.–2:30 p.m. and Sun. 7 a.m.–3 p.m. .

■ Marché d'Aligre

Close to Place de la Bastille, this market has many colorful stalls packed with fruit and vegetables.

Pick up an unusual bargain at Marché aux Puces St. Ouen de Clignancourt.

In nearby Place d'Aligre, a covered market, the **Beauvau,** sells cheeses and *charcuterie* (deli meats and pâtés). There's also a small *marché aux puces*.

Rue d'Aligre and place d'Aligre, 12th arr. • Closed Mon.

■ MARCHÉ BIOLOGIQUE DES BATIGNOLLES

One of Paris's oldest organic markets sells fresh produce and excellent take-out food. Foodies consider this Montmartre market one of the city's best places for great food.

Blvd. des Batignolles between rue des Batignolles and rue Boursault, 17th arr. • Open Sat. a.m.

■ MARCHÉ AUX PUCES ST. OUEN DE CLIGNANCOURT

One of the world's finest markets, in the north of Montmartre, has more than 2,500 shops and stalls spread over a labyrinth of alleyways, selling everything from antiques to scrap. Visit **Biron** *(No. 85)* for high-end antiques, **Serpette** *(No. 110)* for classic furniture, **Paul Bert** *(No. 96)*, which sells the latest in art and collectibles, and **Vernaison** *(No. 99)*—the place to go for everything from toys to textiles.

Rue des Rosiers between ave. Michelet and rue Jean-Henri Fabre, St. Ouen, 18th arr. • Open Sat., Sun., and Mon. • marcheauxpuces-saintouen.com

Le Marais & Bastille

One of the city's oldest and most atmospheric quarters, the area was originally marshland (*marais* means "marsh"). The Middle Ages saw swamps drained and homes erected. During the Renaissance the area came up in the world, and wealthy aristocrats built lavish mansions *(hôtels particuliers)* surrounded by high walls. Nearby was the Bastille fortress, site of the celebrated battle that began the French Revolution. Later the neighborhood went into a long decline, during which many of the grand mansions became derelict. In the 1960s, the Friends of the Marais, aware that a huge part of their architectural heritage was endangered, lobbied City Hall to refurbish the crumbling mansions. Many of the *hôtels* became museums, libraries, and government offices.

❶ **The narrow streets of Le Marais are lined with cafés and restaurants, where you can stop, relax, and people-watch.**

Le Marais & Bastille

From Place de la Bastille, take a stroll through Renaissance Paris via the narrow lanes and stately courtyards of the old Marais.

4 Musée Carnavalet (see p. 102) After renovation, the museum is due to reopen in February 2020. Explore the history of Paris, then continue west along rue des Francs Bourgeois to the Musée Cognacq-Jay.

3 Place des Vosges (see p. 101) Stop to admire what is said to be the most perfect square in Paris. Exit on the northwest side of the square, and walk two blocks down rue des Francs Bourgeois.

2 Hôtel de Béthune-Sully (see p. 100) Stop in at this imposing 17th-century mansion's bookshop, pass through the pretty garden, and go through the doorway into the Place des Vosges.

5 Musée Cognacq-Jay (see pp. 102–103) Admire the 18th-century collection amassed by the founders of La Samaritaine department store. Turn right out of the museum, down rue Elzévir, and left onto rue de Thorigny.

6 Musée Picasso (see pp. 106–107) See some of the 3,000 works by the celebrated Spaniard, as well as Picasso's private collection of works by his peers Matisse, Degas, and Cézanne. Turn right out of the museum onto rue de la Perle, left onto rue Vieille du Temple, and right onto rue des Francs Bourgeois.

PLACE DE LA RÉPUBLIQUE
Ⓜ République
Ⓜ Temple
BLVD. DU TEMPLE
BOULEVARD DES FILLES DU CALVAIRE
Ⓜ Filles du Calvaire
St.-Sébastien-Froissart
Chemin Ⓜ Vert
BLVD.

SQUARE DU TEMPLE
RUE DU TEMPLE
RUE DES ARCHIVES

7 Archives Nationales
8 Musée d'Art et d'Histoire du Judaïsme
Ⓜ Rambuteau
RUE RAMBUTEAU
RUE DU TEMPLE
RUE DES ARCHIVES
Hôtel de Ville Ⓜ

RUE DES
6 Musée Picasso
SQUARE G. CAIN
5 Musée Cognacq-Jay
FRANCS BOURGEOIS
4 Musée Carnavalet
RUE DES ROSIERS
9 The Pletzl

0 — 400 meters
0 — 400 yards

1 Place de la Bastille (see p. 100) Trace the cobblestone outline of the notorious fortress prison where the French Revolution started. Exit on the western edge of the circle, and move down rue St-Antoine.

1 Place de la Bastille

3 Place des Vosges

2 Hôtel de Béthune-Sully

10 Hôtel de Sens

BEAUMARCHAIS

Bastille Ⓜ

BOULEVARD HENRI IV

RUE ST-ANTOINE

BOULEVARD DE LA BASTILLE

BOURDON

Bassin de l'Arsenal

BLVD. MORLAND

Sully Morland Ⓜ

BOULEVARD MORLAND

PONT MORLAND

Quai de la Rapée

PONT DASTRLBLITZ

Seine

QUAI HENRI IV

PORT HENRI IV

PONT DE SULLY

QUAI DES CELESTINS

PORT DES CELESTINS

PONT MARIE

Pont Marie Ⓜ

St-Paul Ⓜ

RUE DE RIVOLI

QUAI DE L'HÔTEL DE VILLE

7 Archives Nationales (see p. 103) Rotating exhibits feature priceless documents and artifacts from France's long and glorious past. Head west along rue Rambuteau and turn right onto rue du Temple.

8 Musée d'Art et d'Histoire du Judaïsme (see p. 104) Jewish art, culture, and history are the focus of this dynamic small museum. Retrace your steps along rue des Francs Bourgeois, turn right onto rue Vieille du Temple, and left onto rue des Rosiers.

9 The Pletzl (see pp. 104–105) Explore Paris's Jewish quarter in this warren of streets, especially along rue des Rosiers. Follow rue Pavée south, cross rue de Rivoli onto rue de Fourcy, and go left on rue de l'Hôtel de Ville.

10 Hôtel de Sens (see p. 105) Now an arts library, this imposing mansion blends Gothic and Renaissance architecture. The back garden provides a great place to relax at the end of your Marais walk.

> LE MARAIS & BASTILLE   DISTANCE: APPROX. 2.1 MILES (3.5 KM)
> TIME: APPROX. 6–8 HOURS   MÉTRO START: BASTILLE

LE MARAIS & BASTILLE

Place de la Bastille

1 The French Revolution went from mere talk to bloody combat when an angry mob stormed the Bastille, a fortified prison and armory, on the afternoon of July 14, 1789. Four hours later the Bastille had fallen, the prisoners held inside were free, and the monarchy was on the verge of collapse. The bastion's former boundaries are traced in cobblestones outside Nos. 5–49 boulevard Henri IV. The **Colonne de Juillet** (July Column)—topped by the golden **Génie de la Liberté** (Spirit of Liberty)—commemorates both the 1789 rebellion and a later uprising in 1830. The striking curved glass facade of the **Opéra Bastille** *(Place de la Bastille, 12th arr., tel 01 40 01 18 50, tours €€€€, operadeparis.fr)*, the more modern of the Opéra National de Paris's two theaters, looms on the southeastern side of the square. The 2,700-seat theater was designed by Carlos Ott and opened in 1989 to mark the bicentennial of the revolution. Guided tours include the main auditorium and the backstage areas.

At the end of rue St.-Antoine, 3rd/4th/11th arr. • Métro: Bastille

Hôtel de Béthune-Sully

2 Built in the early 17th century as a private home and later owned by Maximilien de Béthune, the Duke of Sully, finance minister to King Henri IV, the mansion is one of the city's best examples of King Louis XIII architecture. Now home to the **Centre des Monuments Nationaux** (the National Office for Historical Monuments), caretaker of France's national treasures, it features a bookshop and a garden. The bookshop has a **17th-century ceiling** with painted beams and window embrasures, and carries books in English. From the outer courtyard, decorated with guardian sphinxes and figures representing the seasons and elements, you pass through a porch into the rear garden, which provides a handy shortcut to the Place des Vosges.

62 rue St.-Antoine, 4th arr. • tel 01 44 61 20 00 • Métro: St.-Paul or Bastille • hotel-de-sully.fr

Place des Vosges

3 The early 17th-century town-house mansions that surround the square are noted for their elegant brick facades and long arcades that front trendy restaurants, cafés, boutiques, and art galleries. Built between 1605 and 1612 at the behest of King Henri IV, the square was one of Europe's first attempts at modern city planning and became a template for later developments across the continent. Originally called the Place Royale, although no kings or queens ever lived here, the name was changed during the revolution to honor France's eastern Vosges region: the first to contribute taxes to the new government. Cardinal Richelieu lived at **No. 21** from 1615 to 1627, but the square's most celebrated habitué was the author Victor Hugo. He moved into **No. 6** in the early 1830s, shortly after his novel *Notre-Dame de Paris (The Hunchback of Notre Dame)* became a best seller. His former home is now a museum (see p. 80).

Off rue des Francs Bourgeois, 4th arr. • Métro: Bastille, St.-Paul, or Chemin Vert

Place des Vosges is perfectly symmetrical, with nine houses on each of its four sides.

Musée Carnavalet

4 An ancient recipe for frog's leg soup and Robespierre's farewell letter before facing the guillotine are among the oddities found inside the official historical museum of the city of Paris. The collection is arranged chronologically and sprawls through more than a hundred galleries in two adjacent buildings, the Hôtel Carnavalet and Hôtel Le Peletier de St. Fargeau. The former is a splendid Renaissance mansion, completed in 1548 and later the home of aristocratic letter-writer Marie de Rabutin-Chantal (Madame de Sévigné). A comprehensive look at the city's cultural, intellectual, and spiritual life, the museum covers more than 2,000 years of Parisian history—from the Gauls and Romans through modern times—and ranges from a prehistoric dugout canoe once used on the Seine to the personal effects of Marie-Antoinette. Don't miss the **Sign Galleries,** an unusual collection of street signage from the 16th through the 20th centuries; the reassembled study from the 17th-century Hôtel La Rivière and reception room from the Hôtel d'Uzès; **a scale model of the Bastille;** and various artifacts from the French Revolution including an ornately decorated copy of **The Declaration of the Rights of Man.**

Among the Musée Carnavalet's displays is the re-creation of a room from one of the royal palaces in the reign of Louis XVI.

23 rue de Sévigné, 3rd arr. • tel 01 44 59 58 58 • Closed until Feb. 2020 • Métro: St.-Paul, Chemin Vert, or Bastille • carnavalet.paris.fr

Musée Cognacq-Jay

5 Ernest Cognacq (1839–1928), founder of La Samaritaine department store, began life as a lowly necktie vendor on the Pont Neuf. Even more than his emporium, the museum in his former home shows just how far he climbed during his lifetime. The vast array of paintings, sculptures, jewelry, furniture, and ceramics was amassed by Cognacq and his wife, Marie-Louise Jay, who shared his passion for fine art. The emphasis is on 18th-century France, displayed in the likeminded surroundings of the Hôtel Donon with its exquisite **Louis XV and XVI rooms.** The eclectic collection also contains paintings by Rembrandt, as well as works by Impressionists Paul Cézanne and Edgar Degas. Head up to the attic to see the **exposed roof beams** that let you see how the building was constructed.

8 rue Elzévir, 3rd arr. • tel 01 40 27 07 21 • Closed Mon. and public holidays • Free; temporary exhibitions: €€ • Métro: St.-Paul, Chemin Vert, or Rambuteau • museecognacqjay.paris.fr

Musée Picasso

6 See pp. 106–107.

Hôtel Salé, 5 rue de Thorigny, 3rd arr. • tel 01 85 56 00 36 • Métro: St.-Sébastien–Froissart, Chemin Vert, or Saint-Paul • museepicassoparis.fr

Archives Nationales

7 France's National Archives—one of the few institutions created rather than destroyed during the revolution—are housed in several adjacent 17th-century mansions. Most impressive of these is the **Palais Soubise**, named for the noblewoman and onetime mistress of King Louis XIV who remodeled it (allegedly with the Sun King's funds) into one of the most dazzling residences in the Marais—her apartments show how the nobility lived before the revolution. The archive's treasures are displayed in revolving exhibits in the **Musée des Archives Nationales**. Among the artifacts are the jailer's keys from the Bastille, the only known portrait of Joan of Arc rendered during her lifetime, the **Edict of Nantes** (1598) that granted Protestants the right to worship in France, **Louis XVI's will,** and Marie-Antoinette's farewell letter.

60 rue des Francs Bourgeois, 3rd arr. • tel 01 40 27 60 96 • Closed Tues. and public holidays • €–€€ • Métro: Rambuteau or Hôtel de Ville • archives-nationales.culture. gouv.fr

IN **THE KNOW**

The predominant style of the Marais mansion—or *hôtel particulier*—is a free-standing town house fronted by an entrance court *(cour d'honneur),* where guests and residents would arrive by carriage, and backed by a peaceful garden. Although its roots stretch back to the Middle Ages, the style reached its peak during the Renaissance (15th–17th centuries), when the Marais became a residential quarter for royals and aristocrats, all competing to see who could create the most lavish homes.

Musée d'Art et d'Histoire du Judaïsme

8 The permanent collection runs a broad gamut from ancient Torah scrolls and Hanukkah lamps to modern artworks by Jewish artists from Europe and the Middle East, covering both the Ashkenazi and Sephardic worlds. It also takes in Jewish intellectual and political movements, the diaspora, and Jewish culture during the Middle Ages and Renaissance. The collection is housed in the meticulously restored **Hôtel de St.-Aignan,** built as the city residence of the Count d'Avaux. By the mid 19th-century, the mansion had been subdivided into numerous units, many of them occupied by émigré Jews from Eastern Europe. Among the building's most intriguing features are the rebuilt **grand staircase** and the **dining room** with its recently rediscovered Roman-style grisaille wall decorations.

71 rue du Temple, 3rd arr. • tel 01 53 01 86 53 • Closed Mon., Jan. 1, and Oct. 1 and 9 • €€• Métro: Rambuteau or Hôtel de Ville • mahj.org

GOOD **EATS**

■ **L'AS DU FALLAFEL**
Order this famous Pletzl kebab house's falafel special, which brims with hummus and fried eggplant, and eat it in the street, like the locals do. There is a sit-down section as well. **34 rue des Rosiers, 4th arr., tel 01 48 87 63 60, €**

■ **CARETTE**
This elegant tearoom and café on picturesque Place des Vosges has an extensive menu serving breakfast, lunch, and dinner. Try the velvety hot chocolate and chewy macaroons. **25 Place des Vosges, 3rd arr., tel 01 48 87 94 07, €**

■ **CHEZ JULIEN**
A former turn-of-the-20th-century bakery is now one of the prettiest dining rooms in Paris. In summer, dine on the courtyard terrace with a view of the 16th-century St.-Gervais church. **1 rue du Pont Louis-Philippe, 4th arr., tel 01 42 78 31 64, €€–€€€**

The Pletzl

9 As early as the 13th century, Jews began to congregate in the Marais after they were expelled from the main city. Immigrants from Eastern Europe and Russia arrived during the 19th and early 20th centuries. Despite nearly five years of Nazi occupation and the loss of more than half the population in concentration camps, the neighborhood somehow survived. The name means "little place" in Yiddish, a fitting appellation for the warren of narrow streets that compose today's Jewish quarter. **Rue des Rosiers** is the main thoroughfare, so called because roses were planted here in the Middle Ages. Kosher restaurants and food shops are among the Pletzl's trademarks. The art nouveau-

Kosher bakeries, charcuteries, and other specialist food outlets fill rue des Rosiers in the Marais.

style Orthodox synagogue **Agudath Hakehilot** (*10 rue Pavée*) was designed by Hector Guimard, creator of the wrought-iron entrances of the métro. Dynamited by the Nazis in 1940, it has now been restored.

Rue des Rosiers, rue Pavée, and rue des Écouffes, 4th arr. • Métro: St.-Paul

Hôtel de Sens

10 Created between 1475 and 1507 and one of the few remaining examples of Gothic domestic architecture in Paris, the Hôtel de Sens was originally the lavish pied-à-terre of the archbishops of Sens. Later residents included the scandalous Queen Margot (wife of King Henri IV) and her many lovers. Nowadays the Hôtel de Sens houses an arts library, the **Bibliothèque Forney,** including a collection of historic posters, photos, and postcards.

1 rue Figuier, 4th arr. • tel 01 42 78 14 60 • Closed Sun. and Mon. • € • Métro: Pont Marie or Sully Morland

Musée Picasso

This collection, the world's largest gathering of works by Pablo Picasso, shows what he achieved in decades of artistic innovation.

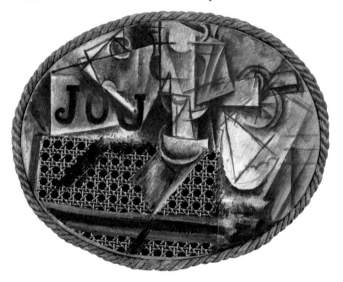

Picasso's cubist work, "Still Life with Cane Chair" (1912), combines paint and collage.

Pablo Picasso (1881–1973) once said, "Give me a museum and I'll fill it," and the Musée Picasso shows that he could do just that. Located in a grand 17th-century mansion in the Marais, the Musée Picasso is filled with pieces that were inherited from the artist's estate in lieu of inheritance tax. The museum, small enough to tour in two hours, provides a distilled and fascinating narrative about the development of modern art through the work of its pioneering Spanish genius.

■ THE STUDIOS

The lower level (Level –1) explores the various studios in which Picasso worked. A photograph taken by Picasso's muse, the photographer Dora Maar, depicts the studio at 7 rue des Grands-Augustins, in which Picasso painted "**Guernica**"(Room 1.3). A selection of prints is displayed around a press from his studio in the villa of La Californie in Cannes (Room 1.6).

■ FEMALE PORTRAITS

On the ground floor (Level 0), a series of female portraits including "**La Celestina,**" and "**Desnudo Sentado,**" shows Picasso's evolving style from 1895 to 1931 (Room 0.3). Next door (Room 0.4), the development of the early masterpiece "**Demoiselles d'Avignon**" is revealed through a group of studies.

■ CUBIST MOVEMENT

Together with traveling companion and fellow artist Georges Braque, Picasso broke through barriers to develop the cubist movement. Both created multiple works on the same subjects, including Picasso's "**Man with Guitar**" and "**Still-Life with Cane Chair**" (Level 0, Room 0.6). On Level 1, "**Guitar and Bottle

of Bass**" and "**Guitar**" are examples of Picasso's organic movement into collage (Room 1.1).

■ RETURN TO CLASSIC PAINTING

After World War I and trips to Italy, Picasso reverted back to a more classic style. "**Portrait of Olga in an Armchair,**" "**Le Retour du Baptême,**" and "**Two Women Running on the Beach (The Race)**" are some of the better known works from this period (Level 1, Rooms 1.2, 1.3, and 1.4).

■ PRIVATE ART COLLECTION

Picasso was an avid art collector. On Level 3, his eclectic private collection includes works by Chardin, Courbet, Renoir, Cézanne, Braque, Matisse, Derain, and Henri Rousseau.

LE MARAIS & BASTILLE

Hôtel Salé, 5 rue de Thorigny, 3rd arr. • tel 01 85 56 00 36 • Métro: St.-Sébastien–Froissart, Chemin Vert, or Saint-Paul • museepicassoparis.fr

Revolutionary Paris

A bankrupt government, food shortages, and discontent among the masses set the stage for revolution; its flashpoint came at the storming of the Bastille on July 14, 1789. From here you can trace the course of the revolution—from the site of the Palais des Tuileries to the Conciergerie, where Queen Marie-Antoinette was imprisoned after King Louis XVI's execution, and on to the place where Madame Guillotine performed her bloody work.

THE GUILLOTINE.

The guillotine (above) was a grimly efficient method of execution. The painter of this view of the storming of the Bastille (right) owned a nearby wine shop and painted what he saw that day.

An Unpopular King & a Popular Uprising

In May 1789, King Louis XVI convened the Estates-General (an advisory body of nobles, church leaders, and citizens) in response to growing public unrest. The citizen leaders formed the National Assembly and pledged not to disband until France had a constitution that guaranteed the rights of ordinary people. The king tried to regain control by banning the Assembly, summoning troops to Paris, and dismissing the popular finance minister, Jacques Necker, on July 11. Three days later, a crowd attacked the Bastille, the king's prison and a symbol of royal authority, looking for weapons and ammunition.

The Fall of the Monarchy

In October 1789, the revolutionaries moved the royal family from Versailles to the Palais des Tuileries (see pp. 118–119). By the summer of 1792, the Paris Commune (which had governed the city since the storming of the Bastille) gained the upper hand over more moderate factions, and from the **Hôtel de**

Ville (see p. 88) revolutionary leaders Danton, Marat, and Robespierre plotted the final, bloody steps—the arrest of the royal family, who were moved to the Temple prison (later dismantled). In 1793, Louis XVI and Marie-Antoinette were executed in the **Place de la Concorde** (see p. 134), along with 2,000 opponents of the revolution.

The Reign of Terror

In fall 1793, the ten-month Reign of Terror began. As many as 40,000 people may have perished. Having dispensed with their enemies, the rebels then turned on one another. In the summer of 1794, moderates sent the last of the Commune to the guillotine, ending the revolution.

BASTILLE DAY
CELEBRATIONS

Bal des Pompiers On July 13, fire stations throughout Paris host fundraising balls. Bands, drinks, and firefighters in full regalia keep revelers happy until the small hours.

Parade On July 14, troops parade down the Champs-Élysées. It's crowded so get there well before the 10 a.m. start.

Fireworks Join the crowds in front of the Tour Eiffel at 10:30 p.m. to see the fireworks display. Arrive by 8:30 p.m. to find a spot.

LE MARAIS & BASTILLE

Signature Dishes

Start the day with a croissant and coffee as you take in the world a few bites and drops at a time. Later on, try some of the best North African cooking outside the Maghreb, or some sweet treats, or that perennial French delicacy, foie gras. End the day with *soupe à l'oignon* at one of the city's always-open brasseries.

■ Viennoiseries

Though these delicacies owe their name to the city of Vienna, there is nothing more Parisian than a buttery pastry. A morning in the Marais is best begun at **Au Levain du Marais** (*28 blvd. Beaumarchais, 11th arr., tel 01 48 05 17 14*), with a croissant whose flaky layers are impossible to count. Or swing through St.-Germain for a *chausson aux pommes* (apple turnover) from **Poilâne** (*8 rue du Cherche-Midi, 6th arr., tel 01 45 48 42 59*). Matcha-green-tea croissants are a big hit at **Du Pain et des Idées** (*34 rue Yves Toudic, 10th arr., tel 01 42 40 44 52*), a popular bakery just north of République.

■ Couscous

The cuisines of Morocco, Algeria, and Tunisia, with their *tagines* (a type of North African casserole) and *merguez* (spicy lamb sausage), are as easy to find here as those of the other regions of France, and often come at a more reasonable price. Two wildly different couscous preparations can be found in the Latin Quarter at **Chez Hamadi** (*12 rue Boutebrie, 5th arr., tel 01 43 54 03 30*) and not far from Pigalle at **Wally Le Saharien** (*36 rue Rodier, 9th arr., tel 01 42 85 51 90*). The former provides a creamy semolina sponge to soak up the juices on top, while the latter's drier, served to the side in a fluffy mound.

■ Petits Fours

In elegant St.-Germain, the *macaron* (macaroon) reaches its highest expression. Those seeking a delicate meringue exterior, thin filling, and classic flavors like raspberry should visit **Ladurée** (*21 rue Bonaparte, 6th arr., tel 01 44 07 64 87*). For fatter, denser cookies with plenty of *ganache* (creamy icing) sandwiched in between, **Pierre Hermé** (*72 rue Bonaparte, 6th arr., tel 01 43 54 47 77*)

LE MARAIS & BASTILLE

Restorative onion soup is a Parisian classic.

is your place. From white truffle to carrot with orange and cinnamon, there is the most adventurous palette of flavors. While here, grab a rum-spiked *canelé* (Bordeaux-style baked custard) or any number of treats that Monsieur Hermé calls *Ispahan*.

■ *FOIE GRAS DE CANARD*
Restaurants high and low around Paris serve infinite variations of this liver delicacy. When the server at St.-Germain's **Chez l'Ami Jean** (*27 rue Malar, 7th arr., tel 01 47 05 86 89*) pulls back the lid of a cast-iron cocotte, he reveals an entire lobe of foie gras, roasted to a lacquered, caramel-

hued brown. For a more dressed-up rendition, **L'Astrance** (see p. 69) marinates the liver in *verjus* (the juice of unripe grapes) and tucks it between slices of raw mushroom on crunchy *brik* dough with hazelnut oil and a puckery lemon confit. A forkful reveals a thousand layers of taste and texture.

■ ONION SOUP
Near the Place des Vosges, **Le Bistrot des Vosges** (*31 blvd. Beaumarchais, 4th arr., tel 01 42 72 94 85*) serves one of the best *soupe à l'oignon* in town, smothered with melted cheese. The bistrot also specializes in meat dishes from the Aubrac region.

The Louvre & Palais-Royal

Between the north bank of the Seine and the busy rue de Rivoli, the Jardin des Tuileries and epic Musée du Louvre are Paris at its most picturesque. They are a fitting home to some of the world's most important art: crowds flock to the Louvre for the enigmatic smile of Leonardo da Vinci's "Mona Lisa" and to the Tuileries's Orangerie to see Claude Monet's paintings of water lilies. On the north side of rue de Rivoli, clothing shops, upscale hotels, restaurants, and souvenir stores do a roaring trade. The arcaded garden of the Palais-Royal, with its mix of boutiques, antiques, and specialists in everything from music boxes to vintage couture, provides an oasis of calm. Next to the Louvre, the royal church of St.-Germain l'Auxerrois offers architectural styles from Romanesque to Gothic.

◖ **The Louvre's pyramidal entrance, designed by architect I. M. Pei, was built in 1986 as commissioned by President François Mitterrand.**

NEIGHBORHOOD **WALK**

The Louvre & Palais-Royal

The Seine's north bank is rich in historic royal palaces and their beautiful gardens, and some of the world's most important art.

❼ Galerie Nationale du Jeu de Paume (see p. 120) This historic tennis court is now a museum of photographic and moving-image art. Walk east on rue de Rivoli, then stroll north on rue de Richelieu.

❽ Palais-Royal (and Le Grand Véfour) (see p. 121) The palace forecourt's boutiques and specialty shops are renowned. Le Grand Véfour is a historic restaurant that still serves great food.

❻ Musée de l'Orangerie (see pp. 119–120) This former palace greenhouse is home to Claude Monet's vast canvases of his lily pond and a significant collection of modern art. Walk to the garden's northwest corner.

❺ Jardin des Tuileries (see pp. 118–119) Spectacular views from the Arc de Triomphe du Carrousel to the Arc de Triomphe and beyond make this a much-loved park. Walk to the southwest corner of the garden.

**THE LOUVRE & PALAIS-ROYAL   DISTANCE: 2.3 MILES (3.7 KM)
TIME: APPROX. 8 HOURS MÉTRO START: LOUVRE-RIVOLI**

THE LOUVRE & PALAIS-ROYAL

Map labels: Concorde, PLACE DE LA CONCORDE, Galerie Nationale du Jeu de Paume, RUE DE RIVOLI, Tuileries, Musée de l'Orangerie, Jardin des Tuileries, PORT DES TUILERIES, QUAI DES TUILERIES, Seine, PASSERELLE LÉOPOLD SÉDAR SENGHOR, PORT DES TUILERIES, PONT ROYAL

114 | WALKING PARIS

❶ St.-Germain l'Auxerrois (see p. 116) This was the parish church of the royal family when the Louvre was a royal palace. Walk north on rue de l'Amiral de Coligny.

❷ Rue de Rivoli (see pp. 116–117) This busy thoroughfare was laid out on Napoleon's orders and links all the sites on this tour. Walk west.

❸ Musée des Arts Décoratifs (see p. 117) See everyday French objects from the 12th to the 20th centuries. Continue to the main entrance of the Louvre.

❹ Musée du Louvre (see pp. 122–125) A medieval fortress that was remade into a Renaissance palace, the building then became a world-class museum. Walk across Place du Carrousel to the garden.

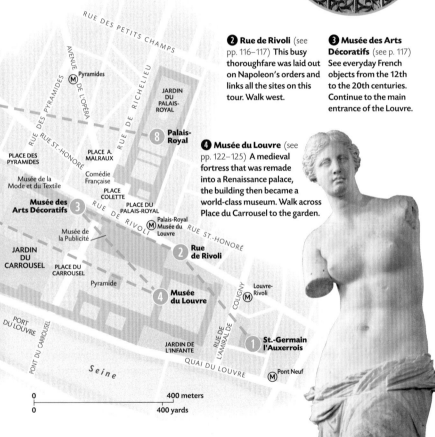

THE LOUVRE & PALAIS-ROYAL

RUE DES PETITS CHAMPS

AVENUE DE L'OPÉRA

RUE DE RICHELIEU

M Pyramides

RUE DES PYRAMIDES

RUE RUE ST-HONORÉ

PLACE DES PYRAMIDES

Musée de la Mode et du Textile

JARDIN DU PALAIS-ROYAL

❽ Palais-Royal

PLACE A. MALRAUX

Comédie Française

PLACE COLETTE

Musée des Arts Décoratifs ❸

Musée de la Publicité

RUE DE RIVOLI

PLACE DU PALAIS-ROYAL

Palais-Royal M Musée du Louvre

RUE ST-HONORÉ

❷ **Rue de Rivoli**

JARDIN DU CARROUSEL

PLACE DU CARROUSEL

Pyramide

❹ **Musée du Louvre**

Louvre-Rivoli M

PORT DU LOUVRE

PONT DU CARROUSEL

JARDIN DE L'INFANTE

RUE DE L'AMIRAL DE COLIGNY

❶ **St.-Germain l'Auxerrois**

QUAI DU LOUVRE

M Pont Neuf

Seine

0 ————— 400 meters
0 ————— 400 yards

St.-Germain l'Auxerrois

1 Many visitors to the Louvre overlook its next-door neighbor, yet this church is one of Paris's architectural highlights. When kings and queens called the Palais du Louvre home during the 14th to the 15th centuries, this is where they worshiped. The church, which predates the palace, was built in the 12th century, although only the foundations of the tower remain from this period. The current medieval architecture is a wondrous mix of Renaissance, Romanesque, and Gothic styles, beautifully embellished with 829 square feet (77 sq m) of **stained-glass windows** from the Renaissance. Much of the original decoration was looted during the French Revolution (when the church was used as a police station and a barn), but it was carefully restored in the 19th century. Highlights include a grand **15th-century Gothic porch** above the west doorway, an **organ** originally commissioned by King Louis XIV for the nearby Ste.-Chapelle (see p. 45), and some exquisitely carved **royal pews** based on designs by French artist Charles Le Brun. The church also has a murky past—its **bells** were rung to signal the start of the St. Bartholomew's Day Massacre (see sidebar on the left).

IN **THE KNOW**

The ringing of **St.-Germain l'Auxerrois's bells** signaled the start of the St. Bartholomew's Day Massacre (August 23, 1572) during the Wars of Religion. More than 3,000 Protestant Huguenots were killed in Paris—and more than 70,000 across France—at the behest of the Catholic Queen Catherine de Médicis and her son King Charles IX.

2 Place du Louvre, 1st arr. • tel 01 42 60 13 96 • Métro: Louvre-Rivoli or Pont Neuf • saintgermainlauxerrois.fr

Rue de Rivoli

2 The covered arches of Paris's main street stretch for 1 mile (1.6 km), from Place de la Concorde (see p. 134) to Place du Louvre, and shelter a rich mixture of cafés, restaurants, elegant shopping, and souvenir shops. Napoleon I commissioned this wide street in 1811 to commemorate his victory over the Austrian army at Rivoli, Italy, in 1797. The arcades have a pleasing classical uniformity and include stores such as **WHSmith** *(No. 248)* —Paris's largest English-language bookshop—and **Galignani**

(No. 224)—the first English bookshop on the continent (founded in 1802, although it settled in its current location in 1856). **Maison Angelina** *(No. 226)* is a perennially popular tearoom famous for its thick hot chocolate. For high-end shopping, try the **Carrousel du Louvre** *(No. 99, inside the Louvre)*, with stores such as Printemps and Lancel. A gilded equestrian statue of the French heroine, **Joan of Arc,** stands at Place des Pyramides, close to where she was wounded in 1429 while fighting the English. Today, the statue is still a place of pilgrimage for French royalists.

From Place de la Concorde to rue St.-Antoine, 1st arr. • Métro: Louvre-Rivoli or Hôtel de Ville

Rue de Rivoli's elegant arcades shelter a selection of designer stores and cafés.

Musée des Arts Décoratifs

3 In the northwestern wing of the Louvre is a museum focusing on decorative French objects. Around 150,000 items from religious and everyday life are on display, including toys, stained glass, furniture, ceramics, and jewelry, all dating from the medieval period to the 20th century. The extensive **doll collection** on the fifth floor is exceptional. Another highlight is the **Galerie des Bijoux**—two rooms, connected by a breathtaking glass bridge, which hold a historic collection of 1,200 rings, necklaces, bracelets, and brooches. The entrance fee includes admission to the adjoining **Musée de la Mode et du Textile,** which has rotating collections exploring the French fashion industry from the 17th to the 20th centuries—including world-famous Parisian haute couture (see pp. 140–141), and to the **Musée de la Publicité,** which tells the history of advertising and has an extensive collection of posters. The café has wonderful views across the Jardin des Tuileries.

107 rue de Rivoli, 1st arr. • tel 01 44 55 57 50 • Closed Mon., Jan. 1, May 1, and Dec. 25 • €€€ • Métro: Palais-Royal – Musée du Louvre • madparis.fr

Musée du Louvre
4 See pp. 122–125.

Rue de Rivoli, 1st arr. • tel 01 40 20 53 17 • Closed Tues., Jan. 1, May 1, and Dec. 25; open until 9:45 p.m. Wed., Fri., and every first Sat. of the month • €€€€ • Métro: Palais-Royal – Musée du Louvre • louvre.fr

Jardin des Tuileries

5 The formal lawns and woodland spaces of this 63-acre (25 ha) garden on the banks of the Seine are all that remain of the Palais des Tuilais, which linked the two wings of the Louvre. Queen Catherine de Médici started the garden in the 16th century. Landscape designer André Le Nôtre, who laid out the park at Versailles for Louis XIV, redesigned the garden in the 17th century, creating the central axis that runs from the Louvre west toward the

You have to be quick to get a chair at the Jardin des Tuileries, especially in summer.

THE LOUVRE & PALAIS-ROYAL

Champs-Élysées. In 1667 the garden opened to the public. Today, with its fountains and ponds, formal flowerbeds, benches and cafés, and numerous statues, including **20 bronzes** by 20th-century French artist Aristide Maillol, it remains a popular oasis.

Atop the **Arc de Triomphe du Carrousel,** at the garden's eastern end, is a striking statue of Napoleon I in a chariot drawn by four horses. Napoleon commissioned the arch in 1806 as an entrance to the Palais des Tuileries and to commemorate his victories. During the 1871 uprisings, revolutionaries torched the Tuileries (the Louvre survived), opening up a superb view known as the **Triumphal Way.** From the Arc de Triomphe du Carrousel you can look west through the gardens to the Luxor Obelisk—a gift from the Egyptian government in the 19th century—in the Place de la Concorde. Or look up the Champs-Élysées to the Arc de Triomphe (see pp. 138–139) and beyond to the Grande Arche de La Défense, 5 miles (8 km) away.

Rue de Rivoli and Place de la Concorde, 1st arr. • Métro: Tuileries

Musée de l'Orangerie

Citrus trees originally grew in the orangerie in the southwest corner of the Jardin des Tuileries, yet it is now more famous for housing Claude Monet's **"Nymphéas,"** a series of eight water-lily paintings. Painted between 1914 and 1918, toward the end of Monet's life, they offer a stunning evocation of the beauty of his garden at Giverny, 43 miles (69 km) west of Paris. The vast scale of the water-lily paintings, exhibited on the top floor, is impressive. Each painting is 6 feet (1.8 m) high, and they are arranged in two groups, one representing dusk, the other, sunrise. They were first put on display when the museum opened in 1927, shortly after the artist's death, and are acknowledged to be among the greatest works of 20th-century art. Following a renovation of the museum in 2006, natural light now washes over these masterworks, with weather playing with the paintings in the way the artist intended.

The museum also houses modern art collected by Parisian dealer Paul Guillaume, including pieces by Pablo Picasso, Francis Picabia, Chaïm Soutine, Marie Laurencin, and Pierre-Auguste Renoir. Highlights include Paul Cézanne's **"Apples and Cookies"** (Room 3) and Henri Rousseau's **"Old Junier's Cart"** (Room 4). The museum also hosts changing exhibitions of 20th-century art.

Jardin des Tuileries, 8th arr. • 01 44 77 80 07 • Closed Tues., May 1, July 14 (a.m.), and Dec. 25 • €€ • Guided tours are held in English Mon. and Wed. at 2:15 p.m. (€€) • Métro: Concorde • musee-orangerie.fr

Galerie Nationale du Jeu de Paume

7 Across the Jardin des Tuileries from the Musée de l'Orangerie, this former indoor tennis court is now used by the Centre National de la Photographie, with exhibits on photography and cinema. Constructed in 1851 by Napoleon III as a copy of the Orangerie, the Jeu de Paume (literally, "game of the palm"— from the time when players hit the ball with the palm of the hand) became a gallery in 1919. In 1986, much of its collection was moved to the Musée d'Orsay (see pp. 154–155) and the new Musée d'Art Moderne (Museum of Modern Art; *11 ave. du Président Wilson, 16th arr., tel 01 53 67 40 00, closed Mon. and public holidays, mam.paris.fr*). After a period of rebuilding, the new Jeu de Paume opened its doors in 2002 with a series of highly popular exhibitions by major figures in the world of photography such as Richard Avedon, Martin Parr, Lee Miller, and André Kertész. The museum shows work by emerging artists and has an international program of collaborative curatorial work.

1 Place de la Concorde, 8th arr. • tel 01 47 03 12 50 • Closed Mon., Jan. 1, May 1, and Dec. 25 • €€ • Métro: Concorde • jeudepaume.org

GOOD **EATS**

■ LE FUMOIR
Chic Parisians come to this large and comfortable restaurant-bar, situated within seconds of the Louvre, for brunch, dinner, or a late-night martini. **6 rue de l'Amiral de Coligny, 1st arr., tel 01 42 92 00 24, €€**

■ LA DAME DE PIC
Award-winning female chef, Anne-Sophie Pic, creates original meals at her trendy restaurant across from the Louvre. Try her signature dish of lobster with red fruit. **20 rue du Louvre, 1st. arr., tel 01 42 60 40 40, €€€€–€€€€€**

■ LE SOUFFLÉ
A restaurant specializing in savory and sweet soufflés that include goat's cheese, artichoke, and haddock, or chocolate and Grand Marnier for dessert. **36 rue Mont Thabor, 1st arr., tel 01 42 60 27 19, €€€**

THE LOUVRE & PALAIS-ROYAL

Palais-Royal (and Le Grand Véfour)

8 This 17th-century palace, originally built for Cardinal Richelieu, has had a tempestuous history. Under the ownership of Louis-Philippe-Joseph, Duke of Orléans, the Jardin du Palais-Royal (Royal Palace Garden) was at the center of Paris's social scene, with merchants, intellectuals, prostitutes, and people from all walks of life—except the police, whom the duke had banned—filling its arcade of shops, cafés, gambling dens, restaurants, and theaters. Today, although smaller than the original built for the cardinal in 1633, the garden retains a formal 17th-century design with lime-tree-lined avenues and a central fountain. While the antiques shops that once dominated the gardens are still there, many have given way to art galleries, perfumeries, shoe shops, and high-end fashion retailers such as Stella McCartney and Rick Owens. The adjacent courtyard boasts a controversial installation of black-and-white striped columns, called **"Les Deux Plateaux,"** by French artist Daniel Buren. The **Comédie Française** *(Place Colette, 1st arr., tel 01 44 58 15 15, guided tours Sat. and Sun., €€–€€€ comedie-francaise.fr),* a state-run theater, has been in the Palais-Royal since 1799. The main palace buildings house government offices and are closed to visitors. The sole survivor of the pre-revolutionary restaurants is **Le Grand Véfour** *(rue de Beaujolais, tel 01 42 96 56 27, closed Aug., €€€€€)* on the garden's north side, founded in 1784 as the Café de Chartres. Brass plaques on the walls mark the preferred tables of French national heroes, Napoleon Bonaparte, Victor Hugo (who ate the same dish for more than 30 years—steak and potatoes with green beans), and Jean-Paul Sartre, among others. The restaurant, run by chef Guy Martin, is now two Michelin-starred.

Garden entrances: rue de Montpensier, rue de Beaujolais/ Passage Perron, rue de Valois, 8th arr. • Métro: Pyramides

Daniel Buren's "Les Deux Plateaux" has become a popular place to relax and have fun.

Musée du Louvre

*Paris's grandest palace holds one of the world's
most significant collections of historic art.*

"Artemis with a Doe" was first displayed at the Louvre when the building was a royal palace.

The Louvre is not only one of the world's great museums, it is one of the
world's great historical sites. The palace was home to medieval kings and,
in the mid-19th century, to Emperor Napoleon III. Although the monarchs
are gone, it has retained the impressive art collections of its former residents.
Today, thousands of beautiful and historically significant works of art are on
display. Despite its size, many visitors flock to its most famous exhibits,
which are often surrounded by a melee of tourists.

■ GREEK ANTIQUITIES

In Room 12 on the Ground Floor of the Sully Wing you'll find the smooth and sumptuously draped curves of the **"Venus de Milo."** Despite the loss of her arms during her almost 2,000-year existence, she is one of the world's most famous antique sculptures.

Next door to the Venus is another monument of ancient Greek art: a section of the Athenian **Parthenon Frieze** (Room 6, Ground Floor, Sully Wing). This extraordinarily well-preserved relief depicts young women participating in a ceremony to honor Athena, goddess of wisdom. The finely carved figures wear robes that are so delicate it is difficult to believe they are made of marble. Best of all, most people rush by the Parthenon fragments on their way to see the Venus de Milo, giving the visitor ample time and space to enjoy a treasure of ancient art.

■ EGYPTIAN & ANCIENT NEAR EASTERN ANTIQUITIES

As with every encyclopedic museum, the mummy- and sphinx-filled galleries are always crowded. A particular highlight of the Louvre's Egyptian collection is **"The God Amun Protecting Tutankhamun"** (Room 26, First Floor, Pharaonic

Egypt), which experts think is a faithful portrait of the young pharaoh.

The museum's collection of ancient Near Eastern Antiquities is perhaps even stronger than its Egyptian holdings. And the artwork here is displayed in galleries that are not filled to capacity with tourists. Room 4 in the Mesopotamian galleries—also called the Cour Khorsabad—is particularly striking. This room features wall reliefs and guard figures from an eighth-century-B.C. wall that surrounded the city of Dur Sharrukin (present-day Khorsabad, northern Iraq). Among these ancient carvings are two enormous **Winged Human-Headed Bulls.** These creatures are 13 feet (4 m) tall and 13 feet (4 m) wide, and would have stood at one of the seven gates to the city. They offered supernatural protection and served an architectural purpose as key structural supports for the gateway and wall.

THE LOUVRE & PALAIS-ROYAL

■ RENAISSANCE ART

The long **Grand Gallery** is the Louvre's main byway, at the center of a network of rooms that contain many of the collection's painted masterpieces. If you approach the Grand Gallery from the staircase housing the ancient Greek statue of Nike, the **"Winged Victory of Samothrace"** (Escalier Daru, Ground Floor, Denon Wing), you will come to Fra Angelico's **"The Coronation of the Virgin"** (Room 3, First Floor, Denon Wing). This glowing, multicolored 15th-century altarpiece was painted for a Dominican monastery near Florence.

Both the diverse crowd of onlookers and the elaborate marble and gilt design will entertain the visitor's eye.

Moving through the gallery, you will likely see a crowd in front of Raphael's charming **"La Jardinière"** (Room 8, First Floor, Denon Wing), a painting of the Virgin playing with the Christ Child and his cousin John the Baptist. Having seen this Madonna, look along the opposite wall for the **"Portrait of Baldassare Castiglione,"** a friend of Raphael and ambassador to the pope from the Duke of Urbino. Castiglione's fur stole is meticulously

In Jacques-Louis David's "The Coronation of Napoleon," the emperor crowns his kneeling wife.

rendered, and his ice-blue eyes are piercing while maintaining a certain warmth. Leonardo da Vinci's **"La Gioconda,"** better known as **"Mona Lisa"** (Room 6, First Floor, Denon Wing), is undoubtedly the Louvre's most famous painting. You will be able to catch a glimpse of the famous smile amid the crowds—but you should also spend time with other magnificent works that do not attract such attention.

◼ FRENCH PAINTINGS

Rooms 75 and 77, accessible through the doorway just behind the "Mona Lisa," are home to the great masterpieces of French neoclassical and romantic art. And while these rooms are crowded, the enormous paintings are large enough for everyone to see. The largest and arguably most dramatic among these is Théodore Géricault's **"The Raft of the Medusa"** (Room 77, First Floor, Denon Wing), which depicts the plight of the victims of a contemporary shipwreck. A group of survivors clings to the raft as it is battered by the waves, and one of them signals with a white cloth at a barely visible boat on the horizon.

The "Mona Lisa" has an entire wall to herself and holds court behind bulletproof glass.

To create this scene, Géricault mixed bitumen into his colors to create deep, dark shadows. Unfortunately, this black wrinkles with time and, despite frequent conservation, the painting gradually becomes darker and less legible.

Other paintings here include Jacques-Louis David's **"Oath of the Horatii"** (Room 75, First Floor, Denon Wing), depicting Roman warriors saluting their father as they are preparing to fight, and Eugène Delacroix's **"Liberty Leading the People"** (Room 77, First Floor, Denon Wing), an eyewitness account of the 1830 revolution.

Rue de Rivoli, 1st arr. • tel 01 40 20 53 17 • Closed Tues., Jan. 1, May 1, and Dec. 25; open until 9:45 p.m. Wed., Fri., and every first Sat. of the month • €€€€ • Métro: Palais-Royal – Musée du Louvre • louvre.fr

Royal Architecture

Despite the execution of the king and his family during the French Revolution, Paris is indelibly stamped with royal buildings. Clovis I, first king of the Franks, established his capital here in A.D. 508, but it was the medieval monarchs who cemented the city's position as a royal stronghold, bestowing palaces and cathedrals on a city whose later inhabitants burned a few down and didn't always seem to appreciate them.

The Bassin d'Apollon fountain at Versailles (above) dates from 1671. The palace's golden fence (right) is a copy, installed in 2008. The original was torn down during the French Revolution.

Island Stronghold

After Frankish kings chose the Île de la Cité as their capital during the Middle Ages, the island became the primary seat of French royalty. All that remains today of the palace that dominated the island are **La Conciergerie** (see pp. 44–45) and the nearby **Ste.-Chapelle** (see p. 45), two of the oldest (and finest) examples of Gothic architecture in Europe.

Royal Expansion

When the throne passed to the House of Valois in 1328, the Île de la Cité's grip on royal affairs waned. King Charles V relocated the royal court to the **Louvre** (see pp. 122–125), a medieval castle that was gradually remade into a Renaissance palace. Charles also commissioned the Bastille (see pp. 100 and 108–109), which four centuries later would play a key role in the city's history, and a royal residence in the Marais, the Hôtel St.-Paul, that no longer exists. Following his example, many of the Valois kings frequented the Marais.

In the mid-16th century, Queen Catherine de Médicis moved the royal court back near the Seine, where she created the Palais des Tuileries and its garden (see pp. 118–119) adjacent to the Louvre.

A Move to the Country

In 1589, the monarchy passed from the Valois to the Bourbons. King Louis XIII continued expansion of the Louvre-Tuileries palace, but in 1624 he built a hunting lodge near a little-known village called **Versailles.** Not much happened with the property until his son assumed the throne in 1643. For a time, the young Louis XIV lived in the Palais-Royal, but he would soon transform Versailles into Europe's greatest palace *(Place d'Armes, Versailles, tel 01 30 83 78 00, closed Mon., Jan. 1, May 1, June 13, Aug. 15, and Dec. 25, €€€€€, chateauversailles.fr).*

NAPOLEON'S **PARIS**

When Napoleon Bonaparte declared himself emperor in 1804, he made the Louvre-Tuileries palace his primary residence. His most conspicuous creation is the Arc de Triomphe (see pp. 138–139), yet he also remade the neighborhood north of the Louvre, creating rue de Rivoli (see pp. 116–117), the victory column in Place Vendôme (made from captured cannon), and La Madeleine church *(Place de la Madeleine, 8th arr.).*

Prêt-à-Porter

Paris is one of the world's premier shopping cities, famous for its elegant style and chic fashion. The city that brought the world haute couture (see pp. 140– 141) also does prêt-à-porter (ready-to-wear) fashion extremely well. For a sample of the best shops in Paris, try on some of these suggestions for size.

■ DEPARTMENT STORES

Paris has some of the world's oldest department stores, as well as some of the most exclusive. Orphaned by Colette, which closed after 20 years of service, Parisian fashionistas can now console themselves at **Nous** (*48 rue Cambon, 1st arr., tel 01 40 28 40 75, closed Sun., nous. paris*), a new concept store founded by former Colette collaborators. The city's oldest department store, **Le Bon Marché** (*24 rue de Sèvres, 7th arr., tel 01 44 39 80 00, lebonmarche.com*) opened in 1838 and features more than 40 designers, including Sandro, Maje, and Dice Kayek, and comprehensive lingerie and beauty sections. Another favorite is **Galeries Lafayette** (*40 blvd. Haussmann, 9th arr., tel 01 42 82 34 56, haussmann. galerieslafayette.com*), which stocks labels such as agnès b, Derhy, and Hugo Boss. It also has good menswear and children's sections. The latest department store to arrive in Paris is a concept shop unlike anything else in the city: **Merci** (*111 blvd. Beaumarchais, 3rd arr., tel 01 42 77 00 33, closed Sun., merci-merci.com*) has loft-style spaces amply stocked with clothes including designs by Stella McCartney and Isabel Marant. There is also an excellent café.

■ INDEPENDENT BOUTIQUES

Heaven (*16 rue du Pont Louis-Philippe, 4th arr., tel 01 42 77 38 89*) is a unique boutique in which designer Lea-Anne Wallis designs and handmakes all the clothes. For whimsical, uplifting clothing, try **Antoine et Lili** (*95 quai de Valmy, 10th arr., tel 01 40 37 41 55, antoineetlili.com*), whose colorful shop contains bohemian designs with exotic influences. **L'Éclaireur** (*40 rue de Sévigné, 3rd arr., tel 01 48 87 10 22, leclaireur.com*) is worth a trip just for the futuristic interior, although the edgy fashion may not appeal to everyone. **Paul & Joe** (*64 rue des Sts.-Pères, 6th arr.,*

Besides its covetable ballet shoes and pumps, Repetto sells a range of exquisite leather goods.

tel 01 42 22 47 01, closed Sun., paulandjoe.com) offers eclectic and very French designs for women, men, and children—plus a makeup line. The trendy menswear section is excellent. **Comptoir des Cotonniers** *(Forum des Halles, Porte Rambuteau, 1st arr., tel 01 56 81 00 18, closed Sun., comptoirdescotonniers.com)* has boutiques all over Paris, offering clothes that are affordable and casually chic. Understated and hip, **Isabel Marant** *(16 rue de Charonne, 11th arr., tel 01 49 29 71 55, isabelmarant.com)* has been producing fabulous fashion since the young age of 15. For simple yet classic

Parisian style, head to **Autour du Monde** *(8 rue des Francs Bourgeois, 3rd arr., tel 01 42 77 06 08, bensimon.com)*, whose Bensimon collection has a line of effortless yet sassy clothing, canvas shoes, perfumes, and accessories.

■ SHOES & HANDBAGS
Repetto *(22 rue de la Paix, 2nd arr., tel 01 44 71 83 12, repetto.fr)* is where the classic ballet pump, the Ballerine Cendrillon, created for Brigitte Bardot, is sold in dozens of colors and fabrics. For exclusive designer handbags head to **Elleme** *(19 Rue Ferdinand Duval, 4th arr., tel 01 43 70 84 59, elleme.com)*.

Champs-Élysées

Running through one of Paris's most prestigious areas in the west of the city center, France's most famous boulevard literally translates as "avenue of the Elysian Fields." The original eastern section was created by Queen Marie de Médicis in 1616, and it is still bounded by celestially inspired gardens. Since extended, this 1.2-mile-long (2 km) tree-lined promenade, which hosts the Bastille Day procession, boasts some of the city's most elegant cafés, shops, and restaurants—making it a favorite place for both Parisians and tourists to go for an evening stroll. The eastern end is anchored by Place de la Concorde, Paris's largest square and site of many revolutionary executions. At the other end stands the colossal Arc de Triomphe—now the site of France's Tomb of the Unknown Soldier from World War I. The ornate Petit Palais and Grand Palais, both built for the 1900 Universal Exhibition, are still used for art shows and events. More fabulous art can be found at Musée Jacquemart-André—a fine example of the area's many ornate 19th-century mansions.

◐ **One of two monumental, 19th-century fountains gracing the Place de la Concorde**

Champs-Élysées

One of the world's most beautiful boulevards has some of Paris's most recognizable sights, as well as street cafés, shops, and fine restaurants.

5 Cathédrale St.-Alexandre-Nevsky (see pp. 135–136) This Russian Orthodox cathedral has an interior decorated with icons, mosaics, and frescoes. Continue on rue Daru, turn left onto rue de Courcelles and then right onto boulevard de Courcelles.

4 Arc de Triomphe (see pp. 138–139) Commissioned by Napoleon I, this monumental arch at the northwest end of the Champs-Élysées honors those who fought for France in the Revolutionary and Napoleonic Wars. Walk east up avenue Hoche, turn left onto rue du Faubourg St.-Honoré and then right onto rue Daru.

Monceau Ⓜ

Parc Monceau

Ⓜ Courcelles

BOULEVARD DE COURCELLES

RUE DE COURCELLES

6

PLACE DES TERNES

Ⓜ Ternes

AVENUE DE WAGRAM

5 Cathédrale St.-Alexandre-Nevsky

AVENUE HOCHE

AVENUE DE FRIEDLAND

RUE DU

Arc de Triomphe

4

PLACE CHARLES DE GAULLE

Ⓜ Charles de Gaulle - Étoile

AVENUE George V Ⓜ DES

CHAMPS - ÉLYSÉES

AVENUE GEORGE V

RUE FRANÇOIS 1 ER

Franklin D. Roosevelt Ⓜ

AVENUE MONTAIGNE

RUE FRANÇOIS 1 E

Alma Marceau Ⓜ

PLACE DE L'ALMA

COURS ALBERT 1ER

PORT DE LA CONFÉRENCE

Seine

CHAMPS-ÉLYSÉES   DISTANCE: 2.9 MILES (4.7 KM)
TIME: APPROX. 8 HOURS   MÉTRO START: CONCORDE

CHAMPS-ÉLYSÉES

6 Parc Monceau (see p. 136) This English-style garden is full of pyramids, pagodas, and other follies of 18th-century landscape design. Leave the park via rue Rembrandt on the south side, turn south onto rue de Courcelles, then east onto boulevard Haussmann.

7 Musée Jacquemart-André (see pp. 136–137) State apartments, private chambers, and a winter garden house exquisite paintings, tapestries, and sculptures of predominantly French, Italian, and Dutch art from the 16th to the 18th centuries.

Musée
Jacquemart-André

BOULEVARD HAUSSMANN

St.-Augustin Ⓜ

Miromesnil Ⓜ

BOULEVARD MALESHERBES

FAUBOURG ST.-HONORÉ

Ⓜ St.-Philippe
du Roule

AVENUE MATIGNON

AVENUE DE MARIGNY

ROND POINT
DES CHAMPS-ÉLYSÉES
MARCEL DASSAULT

0   500 meters
0   500 yards

Champs-Élysées -
Clemenceau Ⓜ

AVE. DES CHAMPS - ÉLYSÉES

Grand
Palais

AVE. FRANKLIN
D. ROOSEVELT

3

Petit
Palais

2

Concorde Ⓜ

1

AVE. WINSTON CHURCHILL

Place de la
Concorde

PONT
DES INVALIDES

PONT ALEXANDRE III

PORT DES
CHAMPS-ÉLYSÉES

PONT DE LA
CONCORDE

CHAMPS-ÉLYSÉES

1 Place de la Concorde (see p. 134) Start at Paris's largest square, where the guillotine worked overtime during the French Revolution. Walk up the avenue des Champs-Élysées, and turn south onto avenue Winston Churchill.

2 Petit Palais (see p. 134) On your left is the smaller of the two palaces built for the Universal Exhibition of 1900. The Musée des Beaux-Arts de la Ville de Paris shows art from antiquity to the 20th century. Cross over avenue Winston Churchill.

3 Grand Palais (see p. 135) The Grand Palais combines three exhibition spaces: Galeries Nationales (temporary art shows), Palais de la Découverte (science museum), and La Nef (grand events), which will all be closed for renovation from December 2020. Return to the Champs-Élysées and head west.

The 75-foot-tall (23 m) Luxor Obelisk was a gift from Egypt in 1826.

CHAMPS-ÉLYSÉES

Place de la Concorde

1 Paris's largest square is bordered by the Jardin des Tuileries (see pp. 118–119), the Seine, and the 18th-century facade of the Hôtel de Crillon. The 20-acre (8 ha) space was created in 1754 to display a statue of King Louis XV. During the French Revolution a guillotine replaced the statue—more than 2,800 people were killed here, including King Louis XVI and his wife Marie-Antoinette. When the square was redesigned in the 1830s, the **Luxor Obelisk,** an ancient obelisk from Ramses II's temple at Luxor, was installed along with two fountains. The **Fountain of the Rivers,** on the north side, represents the Rhône and the Rhine, and the **Maritime Fountain** pays homage to France's seafaring spirit.

Southeast end of ave. des Champs-Élysées, 8th arr. • Métro: Concorde

Petit Palais

2 With a blend of neoclassical and beaux-arts architecture, the "Little Palace" is a work of art to rival the masterpieces held within. The garden portico has frescoes depicting the months of the year and the hours of the day, while French 20th-century artist Maurice Denis painted the portraits of famous artists in the cupola. Visit one of the temporary exhibitions or take your pick of the permanent collection: Greek and Roman antiquities, religious work from the Middle Ages, Renaissance art, 17th-century Dutch paintings, and French work spanning the 18th to the 20th centuries. Highlights include Paul Cézanne's **"Four Seasons"** (Room 8) and Claude Monet's **"Sunset on the Seine in Winter"** (Room 7).

1 ave. Winston Churchill, 8th arr. • tel 01 53 43 40 00 • Closed Mon. and public holidays; Fri. open until 9 p.m. • Temporary exhibitions: some free, some €€ • Métro: Champs-Élysées – Clémenceau • petitpalais.paris.fr

Grand Palais

3 This masterpiece of engineering has it all: beaux-arts architecture, a neoclassical stone facade, ornate art-nouveau ironwork, and a series of allegorical statues. The interior is bathed in light from Europe's largest glass ceiling. The structure was built (along with the Petit Palais) to hold the Universal Exhibition of 1900, with 40 artists creating sculptures, friezes, and other embellishments, such as the **monumental bronze chariots** that take pride of place above each wing of the main facade. **La Nef** (The Nave), at the heart of the complex, hosts major events and art shows staged on a grand scale. The building also includes the **Galeries Nationales** *(ave. Winston Churchill, tel 01 44 13 17 17, €€)*, which holds temporary exhibitions, and the **Palais de la Découverte** *(ave. Franklin D. Roosevelt, tel 01 56 43 20 20, €€)*, a museum and planetarium with displays on math, physics, and other sciences. All spaces will be closed to the public from December 2020 for renovation and upgrade, with La Nef and the Galeries Nationales reopening in spring 2023 and the Palais de la Découverte in spring 2024.

Ave. Winston Churchill, 8th arr. • Closed Tues., May 1, and Dec. 25 • Métro: Champs-Élysées – Clémenceau • grandpalais.fr

Arc de Triomphe

4 See pp. 138–139.

Place Charles de Gaulle, 8th arr. • tel 01 55 37 73 77 • Closed May 8, July 14, and Nov. 11 (a.m.); Jan. 1, May 1, and Dec. 25 (all day) • €€€ • Métro: Charles de Gaulle – Étoile • paris-arc-de-triomphe.fr

Cathédrale St.-Alexandre-Nevsky

5 This striking Russian-Orthodox cathedral was inspired by the church architecture of Novgorod and Moscow. Consecrated in 1861, it was funded by Paris's Russian expatriate community, which had grown rapidly following the defeat of Napoleon I, as well as by a personal donation from Tsar Alexander II. The building takes the form of a cross topped with five golden domes representing Christ and the four Evangelists. The interior is richly ornamented with icons, mosaics, and frescoes, including the fresco in the **central cupola,** which depicts Christ, the Virgin, and numerous saints—the other domes show scenes from the life of Christ. Services are still conducted in Russian.

12 rue Daru, 8th arr. • tel 01 42 27 37 34 • Visits Tues., Thurs., Fri., and Sun. 3 p.m.–6 p.m.; services Mon.–Fri. 9:30 p.m., Sat. 6 p.m., Sun. 10 a.m. • Métro: Ternes or Courcelles

GOOD **EATS**

■ LADURÉE
Elegant tearoom founded in 1862, famous for its pastries and chocolates. It also serves lunch. **75 ave. des Champs-Élysées, 8th arr., tel 01 40 75 08 75, €€€**

■ LE RELAIS DE L'ENTRECÔTE
This steakhouse offers entrecôte steak with a secret sauce, fries, and salad. Seconds are on the house. **15 rue Marbeuf, 8th arr., tel 01 49 52 07 17, €€**

■ MINIPALAIS
Simple, natural dishes served in a refined atmosphere with a magnificent terrace. **3 ave. Winston Churchill, 8th arr., tel 01 42 56 42 42, €€€€**

Parc Monceau

Designed in an English style, complete with follies and other architectural features, this unusual park does not conform to the formal style of most historic French gardens. It was created by Philippe d'Orléans, Duke of Chartres, in 1769 and was transformed into a public park by architect Georges-Eugène Haussmann in 1861. Today, a number of follies remain, including an Egyptian pyramid, a Chinese pagoda, and a Corinthian colonnade alongside an ornamental lake. After strolling in the park, head to the eastern edge to visit the **Musée Cernuschi** (*7 ave. Vélasquez, 8th arr., tel 01 53 96 21 50, closed Mon., Jan. 1, May 1, July 14, and Dec. 25; temporary exhibitions: €€; reopening in March 2020 after renovation works*). This collection of Asian art, originally assembled by 19th-century banker Henri Cernuschi, includes bronzes, ceramics, masks, and other pieces from China, Japan, and Korea—such as a fifth-century **Bodhisattva statue** and a **14th-century Buddha bell**. The museum also hosts temporary exhibitions of Asian art.

Blvd. de Courcelles, 8th arr. • Métro: Monceau

Musée Jacquemart-André

This 19th-century mansion was built by Édouard André and his wife Nélie Jacquemart to house their vast art collection. The

Louis XIV to Louis XVI furniture graces the Musée Jacquemart-André's Tapestry Room.

state rooms contain 18th-century French art, including **"Allegory of Science"** by Jean-Baptiste-Siméon Chardin. Furniture from the Louis XIV to the Louis XVI periods fills the informal rooms, as well as more fine art including the **"Russian Games"** tapestries by 18th-century French artist Jean-Baptiste Le Prince, **"The New Model,"** (circa 1760) by painter Jean-Honoré Fragonard, and "**Christ at Emmaus**" (circa 1628) by the Dutch master Rembrandt. A fresco by Venetian artist Giambattista Tiepolo decorates the winter garden's staircase. The dining room (now the café) also has a Tiepolo ceiling. On the upper floor, the Italian Museum features work from the Italian Renaissance including **"Virgin and Child"** (circa 1465) by Sandro Botticelli, a painting of the same title by Giovanni Bellini, as well as sculptures by Donatello and Francesco Laurana.

158 blvd. Haussmann, 8th arr. • tel 01 45 62 11 59 • €€€ • Métro: Miromesnil, St.-Philippe du Roule, or Saint-Augustin • musee-jacquemart-andre.com

Arc de Triomphe

*Scenes from Napoleon's victories decorate Paris's triumphant arch,
which stands above the Tomb of the Unknown Soldier.*

Traffic races around the Arc de Triomphe day and night.

Paris's most famous landmark after the Eiffel Tower honors those who fought
for France during the French Revolutionary and Napoleonic Wars. Plans for
the triumphal arch began in 1806, following Napoleon I's decisive victory over
the Russo-Austrian army at Austerlitz. The ambitious project was headed by
architect Jean-François-Thérèse Chalgrin; it took two years just to lay the
foundations, and the 162-foot-tall (49 m) arch wasn't completed until 1836.
It is the focal point for France's annual Bastille Day celebrations.

■ Sculptures

France's greatest sculptors of the early 19th century—Jean-Pierre Cortot, François Rude, Antoine Étex, and James Pradier—were commissioned to create works for the arch. The two sculptures on the west facade are **"The Resistance of 1814"** (on the right) and **"The Peace of 1815"** (both by Étex), while on the east facade are **"The Triumph of 1810"** (by Cortot, on the left) and the most renowned, **"Departure of the Volunteers of 1792,"** (by Rude) commonly called La Marseillaise.

■ The Reliefs

The six reliefs on the upper facades represent significant moments of the Revolutionary and Napoleonic Wars: battles at Aboukir, Jemappes, Arcole, and Austerlitz, the fall of Alexandria, and the burial of General Marceau.

■ Top Section

The arcades are decorated with allegorical figures from Roman mythology (by Pradier). Above the frieze of soldiers are 30 shields engraved with the names of major Revolutionary and Napoleonic battles.

IN **THE KNOW**

On August 7, 1919, French Air Force pilot Charles Godefroy flew his Nieuport 11 biplane through the Arc de Triomphe, an event that was captured on newsreels.

The inner facades of the smaller supporting arches list the names of 558 French generals; those who died in battle are underlined.

■ Tomb of the Unknown Soldier

The body of an unidentified French casualty of World War I was laid to rest beneath the arch in 1921. The slab above carries the inscription: "Here lies a French soldier who died for his fatherland 1914–1918." The eternal flame is rekindled every evening at 6:30 p.m. and burns in memory of the dead from both World Wars who were never identified.

■ Museum

An elevator takes visitors up to the attic, where there is a museum on the history of the arch. Another 46 steps bring you to a viewing platform on top of the arch, from which you can enjoy a panoramic view of Paris.

Place Charles de Gaulle, 8th arr. • tel 01 55 37 73 77 • Closed May 8, July 14, and Nov. 11 (a.m.); Jan. 1, May 1, and Dec. 25 (all day) • €€€ • Métro: Charles de Gaulle – Étoile • paris-arc-de-triomphe.fr

Haute Couture

Paris has been synonymous with fine clothes for centuries. Haute couture (literally, "high dressmaking") is centered around the Champs-Élysées, and it is the most exclusive part of French fashion. Its roots are in the exuberant years of the Third Empire under Napoleon III and his wife Empress Eugénie, yet it was an Englishman, Charles Frederick Worth, who forged the present system when he founded his own label in 1854, selling dresses to fashionable ladies.

Chanel (above) has retained its trademark simple look; Jean Paul Gaultier's colorful shows combine high fashion and theater (opposite).

Little Black Dress

Gabrielle "Coco" Chanel opened her first store in 1913, with a revolutionary new style influenced by comfort and simplicity—a sharp break from the corseted clothing that had defined the 19th century. She is best known for the most iconic item ever to grace the catwalk—the Little Black Dress. The color had previously been reserved for funerals, but in 1926, Chanel shocked the fashion world with an elegant, sleeveless design that was cut just below the knee; it was an instant and everlasting success.

The New Look

Following World War II's hardships, fashion during the recovery of the 1950s was defined by Christian Dior's "New Look." Voluminous use of fabric, long skirts, and small shoulders and waists were used to create the classic "hour glass" shape. Dior's elegant, feminine designs captured the world's imagination, and although his dresses were impractical for most women, their influence kept Paris at the forefront of world fashion.

Haute Couture Fashion Shows

Today, haute-couture fashion shows still define the style for the following season. Every spring and fall, the world's press, celebrities, and buyers gather to watch the shows. Not many can afford these clothes, however, as an original can cost hundreds of thousands of dollars.

Putting on a show is often a financial loss-making affair for the fashion houses, yet the publicity gained makes the vast expense of hiring teams of cutters, machinists, embroiderers, and seamstresses—not to mention the cost of the fabrics—worth it. Although the designs are not destined for the mass market, they can set trends which propel a fashion house's prêt-à-porter (ready-to-wear; see pp. 128–129) designs to global acclaim.

FASHION **HOUSES**

Adeline André Founded her fashion house in 1981.

Jean Paul Gaultier Founded in 1976. Jean Paul Gaultier is still the creative force.

Givenchy Founded by Hubert de Givenchy in 1952. Clare Waight Keller is now head of couture.

Stéphane Rolland One of the newest names to join haute couture, with a strong Middle-Eastern influence.

Yves Saint Laurent An assistant to Dior, Saint Laurent founded his own label in 1961 and became one of fashion's biggest names. The current head designer is Anthony Vaccarello.

City by Night

Paris became known as La Ville Lumière ("The City of Light") during the Enlightenment, when it gained a reputation as a center of learning. Early adoption of street lighting—the Champs-Élysées was the first street in Europe to be gaslit—helped cement its nickname. Today, the city is at its most magical after sunset.

CHAMPS-ÉLYSÉES

■ PLACE DE LA CONCORDE

At night, **Cleopatra's Needle** glows pink as the square is gently illuminated by hundreds of old-fashioned street-lamps. As you gaze west down the **Champs-Élysées,** the distant **Arc de Triomphe** (see pp. 138–139) stands out like a beacon against the darkness. To the east, the **Place du Carrousel,** with its own triumphal arch, and to the north, the twin buildings of the **Meurice** and **Crillon** hotels, are all wonderfully lit up. Also aglow is the neoclassical portico of the **Assemblée Nationale** (*126 rue de l'Université, 7th arr.*), home to the lower house of French government, to the south.

■ ÎLE DE LA CITÉ

The pont de la Tournelle on the south side of the Île St.-Louis provides a good view of the city and the **Cathédrale de Notre-Dame de Paris** (see pp. 48–49). Floodlights have been placed around the spires, arches, statues, and gargoyles of this masterpiece of gothic architecture, creating a sense of drama in the darkness.

La Conciergerie (see pp. 44–45), the brooding 14th-century castle where Queen Marie-Antoinette spent her last night before execution, is bathed in beams of light that playfully reflect in the river. Its conical twin towers and imposing stone masonry are vividly lit, making the former prison seem even more dramatic.

■ MUSÉE DU LOUVRE

Both of the Louvre's courtyards (see pp. 122–125) are lit at night, with subtle shadows highlighting the elegance of the building's Renaissance facades. The subdued lighting in the romantic **Cour Carrée** bathes the buildings in soft, warm hues. In the larger **Cour Napoléon,** the I. M. Pei-designed glass pyramid has a magical charm, its translucent form playing with the lights.

Floodlights pick out the detailed gilding on one of the fountains in Place de la Concorde.

■ Tour Eiffel

Since 2000, the tower (see p. 149) has incorporated two illumination systems: the static lighting from 336 600W sodium lamp projectors and the sparkle lighting that runs for five minutes every hour on the hour beginning at 8 p.m. The Champ de Mars provides a good view, but the best one is from the terrace of the Palais de Chaillot *(Place du Trocadéro)*, on the other side of the Seine. From here you have one of the best views in Paris— looking across the river to the Tour Eiffel and the **École Militaire** (see p. 150) beyond.

■ Les Invalides

The golden dome of Les Invalides' **Église du Dôme** (see pp. 151–152) is visible from all along the Seine, but to enjoy its full glory when floodlit, view it from Place Vauban on the south side.

■ Sacré-Coeur

Being constructed of travertine, which remains a weather-resistant white, Montmartre's great basilica (see pp. 168–169) appears to float as on a cloud above the city. If you visit Montmartre at night, take the steps or funicular up to Sacré-Coeur for a panoramic view of the floodlit city.

Tour Eiffel & Les Invalides

Grand landmarks dominate the 7th arrondissement, from the Tour Eiffel and the brilliant gold-topped Invalides to the sprawling 18th-century École Militaire. Occupying a prime position on the banks of the Seine River, the Musée d'Orsay is housed in a former railway station built in 1900. The newest addition to the area, Musée du Quai Branly, boasts a contemporary design that smoothly blends into the surrounding garden. Its rooftop restaurant affords an unparalleled view of the nearby Tour Eiffel. Since the 17th century, the French upper class has gravitated toward the 7th district—the château that now houses the Musée Rodin dates from the early 1700s—and the area is still wealthy today, with quiet apartment buildings, discreet upmarket restaurants, and restrained nightlife.

❍ **Bestriding the Paris skyline, the Tour Eiffel symbolizes the romance of Paris.**

Tour Eiffel & Les Invalides

*The Tour Eiffel and gold-topped Les Invalides
anchor this aristocratic community.*

TOUR EIFFEL & LES INVALIDES

❷ Musée du Quai Branly (see pp. 148–149) **Devoted to non-European art, this museum is located in an original complex designed specifically by Jean Nouvel. Continue on Quai Branly.**

❸ Tour Eiffel (see p. 149) Gustave Eiffel's tower created controversy upon its opening in 1889. Stroll southeast through the Champ de Mars.

❹ Parc du Champ de Mars (see p. 150) A former parade ground is now an attractive garden. Leave at the southeastern end and cross avenue de la Motte Picquet.

❺ École Militaire (see p. 150) The Military Academy was founded by King Louis XV in 1751. Cross Place de Fontenoy.

❻ UNESCO (see pp. 150–151) Modern sculptures are scattered through the UNESCO headquarters' gardens. Walk northeast on avenue de Lowendal.

❼ Les Invalides & Musée de l'Armée (see pp. 151–152) Napoleon's tomb lies beneath the gold-domed chapel. Cross boulevard des Invalides.

**TOUR EIFFEL & LES INVALIDES   DISTANCE: 4 MILES (6.5 KM)
TIME: APPROX. 8 HOURS   MÉTRO START: MUSÉE D'ORSAY**

1 Musée d'Orsay (see pp. 154–155)
The museum specializes in 19th-century art and design. It is rich in Impressionist paintings. Walk west on Quai Anatole France and Quai d'Orsay to Quai Branly.

8 Musée Rodin
(see pp. 152–153) This château museum houses dozens of sculptures by Auguste Rodin.

0   500 meters
0   500 yards

PONT DES INVALIDES

PONT ALEXANDRE III

QUAI   D'ORSAY

PLACE DE FINLANDE

DES MARÉCHAL GALLIENI

Invalides Ⓜ

Seine

QUAI ANATOLE FRANCE

Assemblée Nationale

ESPLANADE

AVE DU INVALIDES

BOULEVARD ST-GERMAIN

1 Musée d'Orsay

La tour-Maubourg Ⓜ

PLACE DES INVALIDES

Solférino Ⓜ

Les Invalides et Musée de l'Armée

7

BOULEVARD DES INVALIDES

Ⓜ Varenne

8 Musée Rodin

JARDIN DE L'INTENDANT

BOULEVARD RASPAIL

Ⓜ Rue du Bac

AVENUE   DE TOURVILLE

PLACE VAUBAN

LOWENDAL

AVE. DE SÉGUR

AVENUE DE BRETEUIL

AVENUE DE BRETEUIL

AVENUE DUQUESNE

St-François Xavier Ⓜ

AVE DE VILLARS

PLACE ANDRÉ TARDIEU

JARDIN CATHERINE LABOURÉ

SQUARE BOUCICAUT

Sèvres-Babylone Ⓜ

BLVD DES INVALIDES

AVENUE DE SAXE

RUE DE SÈVRES

PLACE DE BRETEUIL

Duroc Ⓜ

RUE DE SÈVRES

PLACE HENRI QUEUILLE

Musée d'Orsay

1 See pp. 154–155.

1 rue de la Légion d'Honneur, 7th arr. • tel 01 40 49 48 14 • Closed Mon., May 1, and Dec. 25 • €€€ • Métro: Solférino • musee-orsay.fr

Musée du Quai Branly

2 In a city chock-full of age-old structures and museums, it is unusual to discover a 21st-century museum that blends with its surroundings. At the Musée du Quai Branly–Jacques Chirac, architect Jean Nouvel has achieved this feat through the use of tall glass panels and tiers of multicolored boxes on the exterior and one wall that has been embedded with lush foliage to create a **vertical garden**. The Branly features indigenous art from Asia, Oceania, Africa, and the Americas, including headdresses, masks, statues, totems, costumes, textiles, and musical instruments. As you wander through the exhibits, which are arranged by region, watch for headdresses from

Masks from Southeast Asia in the Musée du Quai Branly

Alaska, sculptures from Mexico, feather tunics from Peru, chest ornaments from India, frescoes from Ethiopia, and a 10th-century **Dogon statue** from Mali. The reservation-only **Les Ombres** restaurant on the top (fifth) floor embraces views of the Seine and the Tour Eiffel.

37 quai Branly, 7th arr. • tel 01 56 61 70 00 • Closed Mon., May 1, and Dec. 25 • €€ • Métro: Bir-Hakeim • quaibranly.fr

Tour Eiffel

3 French engineer Gustave Eiffel built his lofty, cast-iron structure for the 1889 Universal Exhibition on the centenary of the French Revolution. Constructed from more than 18,000 pieces of iron held together with 2.5 million rivets, it was due to be taken down after 20 years. The advent of radio transmission saved it in the early 20th century, as it provided an ideal location for radio antennae. More than 130 years after it was built, the 1,063-foot-high (324 m) tower has become one of the world's most recognized structures. The tower has **three viewing platforms:** You can reach the first two by stairways or elevator. Once there, you'll find panoramic views over Paris—the first level even has a transparent floor—and restaurants, including Michelin-starred **Jules Verne** (tel 01 45 55 61 44, €€€€€, restaurants-toureiffel.com) on the second level. The top platform is reached by elevator only. From here, you can see for 40 miles (64 km) on a clear day, although, in bad weather, you may not even be able to see the ground. At night the Eiffel shines like a beacon, and for five minutes each hour on the hour 20,000 lights mounted on the tower sparkle like twinkling stars.

Parc du Champ de Mars, 5 ave. Anatole France, 7th arr. • tel 08 92 70 12 39 • To second floor and top: €€€€, €€€€€; for stairs: €€€ • Métro: Bir-Hakeim, École Militaire, or Trocadéro • toureiffel.paris

An elevator rises through the Tour Eiffel's intricate network of iron girders. It takes about eight minutes to make a round-trip to the second platform and back.

Parc du Champ de Mars

4 After the École Militaire (Military Academy) was built in the mid-18th century, the land between it and the Seine was named the Champ de Mars and used for military parades and maneuvers. Now, the lovely green space lined with elm trees and benches is used for festivals and special events, such as Bastille Day fireworks displays (see p. 109), and by picnickers and walkers relishing the gardens and views.

Between ave. de la Bourdonnais and ave. de Suffren, 7th arr. • Métro: Bir-Hakeim, École Militaire, or Trocadéro

GOOD **EATS**

■ **LES COCOTTES**
Try a salad, an omelette, or a signature meat or fish casserole in a diner setting near the Tour Eiffel. **135 rue St.-Dominique, 7th arr., tel 01 45 50 10 28, €€**

■ **LA FONTAINE DE MARS**
Classics like *steak frites,* duck confit, and chicken with morels are on the menu at this bistro close to the Tour Eiffel. **129 rue St.-Dominique, 7th arr., tel 01 47 05 46 44, €€€**

■ **THOUMIEUX**
Michelin-starred chef Jean-François Piège has transformed the 1920s art deco brasserie into a hip, luxurious place to be. **79 rue Saint-Dominique, 7th arr., tel 01 47 05 79 00, €€€**

École Militaire

5 King Louis XV started the Military Academy in 1751. An outstanding example of French classical architecture, its central section, with eight Corinthian columns and a quadrangular dome, was constructed in 1773. In 1785, Napoleon Bonaparte trained here and graduated as a second lieutenant. During the Second Empire, the addition of two wings made for a sprawling complex. From Place de Fontenoy, you can see the Cour d'Honneur flanked by porticoes with twinned columns. The buildings now house military training facilities.

1 place Joffre, 7th arr. • tel 01 73 71 36 95 • No visits inside the building • Métro: École Militaire

UNESCO

6 In a true international meeting of minds, a group of three architects—from France, Italy, and the United States—designed the UNESCO Headquarters building. Opened in November 1958, the main building's layout is based on a Y, or three-pointed star. Sculptor Isamu Noguchi created the **Peace Garden,** donated by

The golden dome of the Église du Dôme rises above the main courtyard of Les Invalides.

the Japanese government. Paths meander past dwarf trees, stands of bamboo, flower beds, and ponds all designed to resemble Japan's natural landscape. Wandering through the grounds, you come across large works of art, such as **"The Fall of Icarus"** by Pablo Picasso, painted on wood panels mounted on a large wall. The Russian Federation gifted Zurab Tsereteli's egg-shaped sculpture **"Birth of a New Man"** to commemorate the 500th anniversary of Christopher Columbus's voyage to the Americas.

7 place de Fontenoy, 7th arr. • tel 01 45 68 10 00 • Closed Sat. and Sun. • Access is limited to the library • Métro: Ségur, Cambronne, or École Militaire • unesco.org

Les Invalides and Musée de l'Armée

In 1670, King Louis XIV founded the Hôtel des Invalides as a hospital and home for invalid soldiers, and commissioned the gold-domed chapel, the **Église du Dôme,** for the use of the royal family. Completed in 1706, the chapel is a masterpiece of French classical architecture and houses **Napoleon's tomb.** Napoleon's ashes were brought from St. Helena in 1840, and in 1861 they were placed in six nested coffins inside a massive red quartzite encasement, which stands on a pedestal of dark green granite. Twelve giant figures, representing Napoleon's military victories, surround the tomb. Les Invalides once housed 7,000 veterans. Far fewer live there now, and most of the rooms are given over to a group of military museums. In the Musée de l'Armée, which traces the history of armies from medieval times to today, look for medieval armor and artillery models. The **Musée de l'Ordre de la Libération** has displays devoted to the work of the Resistance from 1940 to 1944. The **Musée des Plans-Reliefs** shows relief maps and model fortresses.

129 rue de Grenelle, 7th arr. • tel 08 10 11 33 99 or 01 44 42 38 77 • Closed Mon., Jan. 1, May 1, and Dec. 25• One ticket provides access to the Église du Dôme, the Musée de l'Armée, the Musée des Plans-Reliefs, and the Musée de l'Ordre de la Libération: €€ • Métro: La Tour-Maubourg or Varenne

SAVVY **TRAVELER**

Between Les Invalides and the Tour Eiffel, pedestrian-friendly **rue Cler** teems with fresh fruit, vegetables, fish, meat, and cheese markets, and tempting patisseries. Behind UNESCO, the **avenue de Saxe** market *(Thurs., Sat.)* brims with vendors selling clothing, jewelry, leather bags, farm-fresh produce, meat, and fish. Listen out for the men bursting into song while throwing their fish back and forth—all in good fun.

Musée Rodin

8 The naturalism, flowing lines, and emotion of Auguste Rodin's sculptures have shocked and delighted audiences in equal measure, and many of these great works now fill the rooms and grounds of the 18th-century Hôtel Biron. At the turn of the 20th century, this rococo-style château provided a temporary residence and workplace for artists Henri Matisse and Jean Cocteau, dancer Isadora Duncan, and Rodin himself. The building—recently renovated and now with additional exhibition rooms—houses works from all stages of Rodin's career, plaster models of many of his best-known sculptures, and a display on the bronze casting process. Highlights include one of his first major works, **"The Bronze Age,"**

a figure of a youth that is so lifelike it scandalized the public of the day, a version of "**The Kiss**," and the unfinished "**Thought**." Wandering the tranquil, flower-filled garden, you can find several of Rodin's monumental sculptures. "**The Gates of Hell**" is an unfinished bronze door decorated with scenes from Dante's *Inferno*. A small-scale, early version of "The Thinker" appears above the door panels. Nearby, you can see a full-size version of "**The Thinker**," which Rodin originally entitled "The Poet" because it represents Dante. Also in this part of the garden, "**The Burghers of Calais**" commemorates the six burghers who surrendered the keys of the city of Calais to King Edward III of England in 1347, after a year-long siege. This group memorial captures a range of emotions from despair to defiance.

79 rue de Varenne, 7th arr. • tel 01 44 18 61 10 • Closed Mon., Jan. 1, May 1, and Dec. 25 • €€€ • Métro: Varenne or Invalides • musee-rodin.fr

Many of Rodin's sculptures are exhibited in the museum gardens.

Musée d'Orsay

The museum is famous for its unparalleled collection of Impressionist paintings.

TOUR EIFFEL & LES INVALIDES

The main hall of the former railway station is now a light-filled sculpture gallery.

The Musée d'Orsay features European painting, sculpture, drawing, decorative arts, and photography made between 1848 and 1914. Formed in the 1980s from the holdings of other major French museums, the collection is a greatest-hits feast of Édouard Manet, Claude Monet, Paul Cézanne, Vincent van Gogh, and other superstars alongside equally magnificent works by their lesser-known contemporaries. The museum also has a fascinating design collection and temporary exhibitions.

THE NAVE

The 128-foot-high (39 m) main hall of the former railway station with its arched vault provides a perfect setting for the museum's sculpture collection. Don't miss Jean-Baptiste Carpeaux's **"Dance,"** which caused a scandal when it was first shown, Edgar Degas's **"Small Dancer, Aged 14,"** and Auguste Rodin's **"Balzac."**

SNAPSHOTS OF MODERN LIFE

The newly refurbished rooms on Level 5 display work by the Impressionists. While Edgar Degas is best known for his pictures of ballerinas (plenty of which can be found here), his **"In a Café"** (aka "The Absinthe Drinker") provides a realistic and haunting picture of Parisian bars at the end of the 19th century.

The happier side of bourgeois Parisian social life is on display in Pierre-Auguste Renoir's **"Dance at Le Moulin de la Galette,"** in which couples clad in a symphony of blues dance outdoors amid glowing lanterns. Another wonderful rendering of the late 19th century's Golden Age is on display in James Tissot's **"Evening"** (1885), an ode to extravagant fin-de-siècle evening gowns.

BEGINNINGS OF MODERN ART

The museum is home to one of Édouard Manet's most famous and scandalous works, **"Luncheon on the Grass"** (Level 5). The painting of art students picnicking alongside a naked woman, in a contemporary rather than allegorical setting, has been copied and referenced by Pablo Picasso and dozens of other painters. Among the many works by Claude Monet (Level 5) is **"Rouen Cathedral: Blue and Gold Harmony, Bright Sunlight."**

Some highlights among the Postimpressionists on Level 5 include Cézanne's **"The Card Players"** and **"Apples and Oranges,"** examples of Cézanne's late works, which influenced the cubists. Also look out for Vincent van Gogh's **"The Church at Auvers"** and a version of **"Bedroom in Arles."**

1 rue de la Légion d'Honneur, 7th arr. • tel 01 40 49 48 14 • Closed Mon., May 1, and Dec. 25 • €€€ • Métro: Solférino • musee-orsay.fr

Impressionists in the City

At their first exhibition in Paris in 1874, the Impressionists caused outrage. Claude Monet, Auguste Renoir, Camille Pissarro, Alfred Sisley, and their friends had torn up centuries of tradition that aimed to reproduce the visual world in intricate, accurate detail. Instead they painted quickly and freely, using dabs of vivid color. Their aim was to capture the moment, to paint a spontaneous response to the reality that they saw around them. And one of their prime subjects was Paris.

Auguste Renoir (above) at work out of doors around 1910; his "Dance at Le Moulin de la Galette" (right)

Modern Life

Impressionists rejected the historical and allegorical subject matter of the time, wanting to paint their own world: bourgeois, metropolitan, pleasurable. Paris was still undergoing Baron Haussmann's massive replanning (see p. 8–9), opening up grand boulevards and putting in gas lighting, tramlines, piped water, and sewers. The Impressionists caught the energy of a city on the move.

In Search of Subject Matter

The Impressionists liked to work outdoors. In 1869, Monet and Renoir went to a popular bathing place called La Grenouillère at Croissy-sur-Seine, west of Paris, to depict Parisians at play, boating and bathing; it also proved the perfect location for testing their painting technique on the flickering effects of light on water. Monet was also attracted to industrial scenes and in 1876 and 1877 made a series of studies at the Gare St.-Lazare, recording the steam, energy, and activity of a busy Paris railway station. Renoir was drawn to restaurants and the outdoor dance-café at the Moulin de la Galette in Montmartre. Pissarro painted the city's busy streets and bridges filled with horse-drawn traffic. Sisley painted barges on the Seine.

The Path to Fame

Within 20 years Impressionism had been accepted, and other artists took the experiment in different directions. Henri de Toulouse-Lautrec brought a new, more decadent vision to the dance halls and bars of Paris, while Georges Seurat applied his pointillist technique to Parisian subjects. For the power to communicate contemporary Parisian life across the centuries, nothing quite matches the work of the Impressionists during the 1870s.

IMPRESSIONIST TECHNIQUE

Several of the Impressionists worked out of doors in order to study the changing effects of light and weather. They tried out new types of composition, painting subjects from unusual angles or cropping parts out. To create luminosity across the whole canvas, they applied the paint in individual strokes and dabs of color, rather than mixing colors on the palette and blending brushstrokes together. And they suggested figures and forms rather than painting them in detail.

Cafés & Brasseries

A good reason to go to Paris is to sit in a café and let the hours drift by as you sip coffee and write your next novel, or people-watch, or daydream. Or relax over a beer or glass of wine in a brasserie; these small restaurants traditionally have beer on tap and serve single dishes or larger meals all day.

■ People-watching Cafés

Café Constant (*139 rue St.-Dominique, 7th arr., tel 01 47 53 73 34*), close to Les Invalides, serves above-par food for a local café thanks to its award-winning chef. Named for the exquisite horseshoe-shape zinc bar that dominates the room, **Le Petit Fer à Cheval** (*30 rue Vieille du Temple, 4th arr., tel 01 42 72 47 47*) is a great place for *un verre* and watching the cast of Marais characters wandering in and out.

In the non-touristy part of Montmartre, **Le Sancerre** (*35 rue des Abbesses, 18th arr., tel 01 42 58 08 20*) is the bar/café for watching the neighborhood locals and the Montmartre artists and hipsters. Open daily, it gets crowded at lunch and in the late evening.

Chez Prune (*36 rue Beaurepaire, 10th arr., tel 01 42 41 30 47*) is the bohemian bistro that helped turn the Canal St.-Martin area hip. The *steak frites* are among the city's best, as is the people-watching, which comes with a view of the canal.

■ Iconic Cafés

The chic **Café de Flore** (*172 blvd. St.-Germain, 6th arr., tel 01 45 48 55 26*) has been a fixture on the busy boulevard St.-Germain since it opened in the late 1800s, and the café's ambience and art deco interior haven't changed much over the years. Located around the corner is the more famous **Les Deux Magots** (*6 place St.-Germain-des-Prés, 6th arr., tel 01 45 48 55 25*). These two cafés, frequented by the intellectuals of the 1950s and 1960s, including Jean-Paul Sartre and Simone de Beauvoir, are well known and expensive.

■ Historic Cafés

Order a coffee or a glass of champagne at **Café de la Paix** (*5 place de l'Opéra, 9th arr., tel 01 40 07 36 36*) and linger

Historic Café de Flore is still a popular place to meet friends and relax.

at this beautiful terrace café. Both the café and its regal neighbor, the Opéra Garnier, were designed by architect Charles Garnier. The waiters can be brusque, but the place is steeped in history and dripping with glamour. **Lipp** *(151 blvd. St.-Germain, 6th arr., tel 01 45 48 53 91)* is more than a brasserie—it's a piece of Paris history. In the mid-20th century, Lipp drew influential people, just like its St.-Germain near-neighbors Flore and Les Deux Magots. You might still glimpse a senator or a celebrity lunching or drinking at Lipp, originally an 1880s brasserie offering beer and choucroute.

■ CLASSIC BRASSERIES

The muses of the four seasons—a classic art nouveau motif—decorate the walls of **Julien** *(16 rue du Faubourg St.-Denis, 10th arr., tel 01 47 70 12 06)*. The service is thoughtful and attentive, and for dessert the hot Valrhona chocolate sauce served with a flourish on profiteroles is dreamy. Situated at the tip of Île St.-Louis, the classic **Brasserie de l'Île St.-Louis** *(55 quai de Bourbon, 4th arr., tel 01 43 54 02 59)* from 1870 is still family-owned, with cold beer on tap year-round and mulled wine *(vin chaud)* in winter. The terrace has views of the back of Notre-Dame.

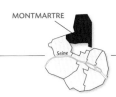

Montmartre

Perched on a hilltop known as La Butte, Montmartre in northern Paris has always stood apart from the rest of the city. Yet it captures the essence of Old Paris like no other neighborhood. Its signature landmark is the magnificent Basilique du Sacré-Coeur—a great starting point for any first-time visitor—but it's in the winding streets that slope down from the basilica that this hilltop enclave shows its real character. The cobblestone roads with their romantic street lamps evoke a sense of the late 19th century, when artists flocked to this once tiny village that became synonymous with high bohemian living. Follow in the footsteps of its famous residents at the Place du Tertre, where Pablo Picasso once painted, and the Moulin de la Galette, the windmill immortalized by painter Pierre-Auguste Renoir, and as you stroll along the gorgeous avenue Junot. Of course, Montmartre can be a tourist trap, but take time out among its squares and hills and you'll still feel its bohemian pulse.

◀ **Montmartre's atmospheric streets have been the setting for films such as *Moulin Rouge!* and *La Vie en Rose.***

Montmartre

On this walk through Montmartre's old streets, from the Basilique du Sacré-Coeur to the Moulin de la Galette, you'll get a real taste of the area's villagey feel.

1 Basilique du Sacré-Coeur
(see pp. 168–169) Climb up into the dome of this famous Parisian landmark for breathtaking views of the city. Outside, head west to rue Azaïs, then turn right onto rue du Mont Cenis.

2 St.-Pierre de Montmartre
(see p. 164) Discover one of Paris's oldest churches, built on the site of an ancient Roman temple. Outside, head west on rue Norvins, then turn left.

3 Place du Tertre (see pp. 164–165) This pretty square, with its street artists and colorful cafés, is a great place to people-watch. Head north on rue du Mont Cenis, and turn left onto rue Cortot.

Map labels:
BOULEVARD NEY
PORTE DE MONTMARTRE
BOULEVARD ORNANO
Porte de Clignancourt (M)
Simplon (M)
Jules Joffrin (M)
Marcadet Poissonniers (M)
RUE CHAMPIONNET
RUE ORDENER
RUE CUSTINE
SQUARE LÉON SERPOLLET
Lamarck (M)
Musée de Montmartre 4
Basilique du Sacré-Coeur
St.-Pierre de Montmartre 2 1
SQUARE WILLETTE
Château Rouge (M)
BOULEVARD BARBÈS
Barbès Rochechouart (M)
Avenue Junot 5
Place du Tertre 3
Abbesses (M)
Moulin de la Galette 6
RUE CAULAINCOURT
BOULEVARD CHAMPIONNET
RUE DE CLICHY
Blanche (M)
Place de Clichy (M)
BLVD DE CLICHY
Porte de St.-Ouen (M)
SQUARE CARPEAUX
Guy Môquet (M)
CIMETIÈRE DE MONTMARTRE
La Fourche (M)
AVENUE DE CLICHY
AVENUE DE ST.-OUEN

7 Musée Gustave Moreau (see p. 167) This museum, adapted from Gustave Moreau's family home, houses more than 7,000 works of art by the symbolist artist.

4 Musée de Montmartre (see p. 165) Find out all you need to know about the history of Montmartre and the lives of its most famous residents in this quirky little museum. Walk west on rue Cortot, cross rue des Saules, and continue west on rue de l'Abreuvoir. Turn north on rue Girardon and left onto avenue Junot.

5 Avenue Junot (see p. 166) Soak up the atmosphere of this elegant, leafy street with gracious houses and artists' studios. Turn south on rue Girardon.

6 Moulin de la Galette (see p. 166) Montmartre's two remaining windmills were immortalized by painters Pierre-Auguste Renoir and Vincent van Gogh. Head west on rue Lepic, turn left at boulevard de Clichy, right down rue de Pigalle and onto rue de La Rochefoucauld.

> 600 meters
> 600 yards

MONTMARTRE

MONTMARTRE DISTANCE: APPROX. 1.6 MILES (2.5 KM)
TIME: APPROX. 6–8 HOURS MÉTRO START: ABBESSES OR ANVERS

Basilique du Sacré-Coeur

1 See pp. 168–169.

Parvis du Sacré-Coeur, 18th arr. • tel 01 53 41 89 00 • Open every
day 6 a.m.–10:30 p.m. • Dome and crypt: € • Métro: Abbesses or Anvers (then the
funicular railway from Funiculaire Gare Basse; you can use a standard métro ticket) •
sacre-coeur-montmartre.com

St.-Pierre de Montmartre

2 Dwarfed by the great Sacré-Coeur basilica opposite, St.-Pierre
has none of the opulence of its grander neighbor, but there's
still plenty to see. This simple church is Paris's second oldest
(after St.-Germain-des-Prés; see p. 74) and is all that remains of
Montmartre's Benedictine abbey, founded by King Louis VI and his
wife, Adélaïde de Savoie, its first abbess, in 1133. The last abbess was
guillotined during the revolution and the abbey was closed. It was
reconsecrated in 1908. There have been many renovations over the
years, but original features include the 12th-century **vaulted choir**

and four **marble columns** said to have come from a
Roman temple that once stood on the site. The northern
aisle contains the **tomb of Adélaïde de Savoie**. If you
are passing by on November 1, you can visit the tiny
adjoining cemetery—the oldest in Paris—which opens
on this one day only. It houses the graves of sculptor
Jean-Baptiste Pigalle and explorer Louis de Bougainville,
who gave his name to the shrub bougainvillea.

2 rue du Mont Cenis, 18th arr. • tel 01 46 06 57 63 • Métro: Abbesses
or Anvers (then the funicular railway from Funiculaire Gare Basse)

**St.-Pierre de Montmartre's
modern stained-glass
windows date from 1953.**

Place du Tertre

3 Montmarte's pretty tree-lined square is the historic
heart of bohemian Paris, where artists including
Claude Monet, Pierre-Auguste Renoir, and Pablo
Picasso once painted. Today, it's full of street artists,
expensive cafés, and tourists, but some of the area's

original spirit remains in its old buildings. **À la Mère Catherine** (*No. 6, tel 01 46 06 32 69, €€, lamerecatherine.com*) is said to be Paris's oldest bistro: Following the 1814 Battle of Paris, Cossack soldiers who ate here would shout *"Bistro!"* (Russian for "Quick!"), inadvertently creating a new kind of Parisian restaurant. The house at **No. 21** was once the home of the Montmartre Free Commune, founded in 1920 to preserve the free-thinking spirit of the area. The commune proposed a number of eccentric policies, including banning December, January, and February, and limiting the number of tourists visiting the area. Ironically, the building now houses the tourist office.

Place du Tertre, 18th arr. • Métro: Abbesses or Anvers (then the funicular railway from Funiculaire Gare Basse)

Musée de Montmartre

4 This showcase of Montmartre's cultural and historical life is located in a 17th-century house—the oldest in the area. From 1875 onward, it was converted into studios that were used by artists Renoir, Raoul Dufy, Maurice Utrillo, and Suzanne Valadon. Today, the lower floors are devoted to displays about Montmartre's history through France's revolutions and wars, while the upper floors evoke the hedonistic days of the area's artistic life. Highlights include a reconstruction of Utrillo's favorite café, **L'Abreuvoir**, the original painted sign of the famous local cabaret, **Au Lapin Agile**, and artworks by Utrillo, Dufy, and Henri de Toulouse-Lautrec. Also don't miss a reproduction of novelist Roland Dorgelès's hoax painting, **"Sunset over the Adriatic"** (1910), which was acclaimed by the critics until he revealed that he and a group of friends had produced it by attaching a brush to a donkey's tail in a satirical attack on modern art.

12 rue Cortot, 18th arr. • tel 01 49 25 89 39 • Open every day; Jan. 1 and Dec. 25 from 11:30 a.m. • €€ • Métro: Anvers (then the funicular railway from Funiculaire Gare Basse)

GOOD **EATS**

■ **BISTRO POULBOT**
This bistro behind Sacré-Coeur serves classic French food with a twist. **3 rue Pulbot, 18th arr., tel 01 42 23 32 07, €€–€€€**

■ **LE COQ RICO**
Come share Chef Antoine Westermann's passion for poultry—his Bresse chicken is a must. Check out the *plat du jour* from Mon. to Fri., for only €15. **98 rue Lepic, 18th arr., tel 01 42 59 82 89, €–€€€**

MONTMARTRE

Avenue Junot

5 A century ago, avenue Junot was part of a scrubby, overgrown area of maquis inhabited by vagrants. Now it is the last word in chic, with an elegance and exclusivity that has earned it the nickname "Champs-Élysées of Montmartre." This broad, tree-lined thoroughfare, home to wealthy Montmartrois, is graced with fabulous private houses and painters' studios. Look in particular for: **No. 13,** the former home of the early 20th-century illustrator Francisque Poulbot, known for his drawings of street urchins (you can see his colorful mosaics of children outside the house); **No.15,** the cubist house of the Romanian poet and founder of dadaism, Tristan Tzara, designed by the architect Adolf Loos; and, at **No. 23 bis,** the Villa Léandre, a group of fairy-tale art deco houses with beautiful gardens.

Ave. Junot, 18th arr. • Métro: Lamarck

Moulin de la Galette

6 One of Montmartre's two remaining wooden windmills (there were once 14), the Moulin de la Galette on rue Lepic was built in 1622, when it was known as the Blute-fin. Originally just a humble mill used to press grapes and grind grain, it had a change of fortunes in the 19th century, when the Debray family bought it and used it to make a type of rye bread called *galette*. The bread, served with a glass of milk, became so popular that the mill's name was changed to Moulin de la Galette. Over the years the Debrays replaced the milk with wine, and by the end of the century the mill had become a hugely popular dance hall and the center of Paris's social scene. It was immortalized by artists such as Vincent van Gogh and, most notably, Pierre-Auguste Renoir, whose "Dance at Le Moulin de la Galette" (see pp. 155, 157) now hangs in the Musée d'Orsay (see pp. 154–155). Today the Moulin de la Galette is closed to the public. Nearby on rue Lepic, the **Moulin Radet,** another mill owned by the Debrays, towers above a modern restaurant called **Moulin de la Galette.**

Rue Lepic, 18th arr. • Métro: Lamarck

Moulin Radet, built in 1717 on a nearby site, moved to its current location in 1924.

Musée Gustave Moreau

This little-visited museum dedicated to the fantastical works of symbolist painter Gustave Moreau (1825–1898) holds an astonishing legacy of 1,000 of his oil and watercolor paintings, plus 7,000 drawings and a superb collection of his unfinished sketches. The gallery is in the home that Moreau shared with his parents; he designed it himself to display his works in the way he wanted. The collection includes **"Apollo and Pegasus"** and **"The Unicorns."** Both paintings demonstrate the artist's fascination with mythology, which he depicted with vivid swirls of color. You can also see the Moreau family's small apartment rooms, which are crammed with personal belongings and furniture, and Moreau's study and collection of rare books.

14 rue de la Rochefoucauld, 9th arr. • tel 01 48 74 38 50 • Closed Tues., Jan. 1, May 1, and Dec. 25 • €€ • Métro: Trinité • musee-moreau.fr

MONTMARTRE

Basilique du Sacré-Coeur

Perched on top of Montmartre, the magnificent Basilica of the Sacred Heart was built as a symbol of national reconciliation and hope.

You can avoid the 225 steps up to Sacré-Coeur by taking the funicular railway.

This landmark church, built to symbolize the return of France's self-confidence after its defeat in the 1871 Franco-Prussian war, is dedicated to the Sacred Heart of Jesus. The basilica was built atop the hill because, according to legend, St. Denis—the city's patron saint—was martyred there. Construction began in 1875 with a Romano-Byzantine design by architect Paul Abadie, and it took 39 years to complete. The 272-foot-high (83 m) structure is built from travertine, a form of limestone that bleaches with age, so the church retains its pale color.

◼ FACADE

Above the facade's triple-arched portico are **bronze statues of Joan of Arc and St. Louis,** and above them stands a **statue of Christ**. The bronze doors illustrate scenes from the life of Christ.

◼ INTERIOR

The vast interior is decorated with mosaics, the most stunning of which—the **"Great Mosaic of Christ in Majesty"** designed by Luc-Olivier Merson and Marcel Magne (1912–1922)—is also one of the world's largest. Other highlights include the Renaissance-style silver statue of the **"Virgin Mary and Child"** by P. Brunet (1896) in the ambulatory, **stained-glass windows** by Fernand Léger, and a magnificent pipe organ built by Aristide Cavaillé-Coll.

◼ DOME

The top of the central dome is the second highest point in Paris after the Tour Eiffel (see p. 149) and has breathtaking, panoramic views stretching for more than 30 miles (48 km). To reach it, you must walk up a 300-step spiral staircase.

(see p. 149)

IN **THE KNOW**

Although the basilica was built on the general theme of recovery and hope, it also contains several nationalist themes. Joan of Arc and St. Louis, who appear in statues above the portico, are both French national saints, and the Savoyarde bell, cast in 1895 in Annecy, is a reference to the annexation of Savoy by French troops in 1860.

◼ BELL TOWER

The 252-foot-high (77 m) octagonal bell tower contains one of the world's heaviest bells; the 10-foot-high (3 m) **Savoyarde** weighs in at 20.4 tons (18.5 tonnes)—the clapper alone weighs 1,900 pounds (850 kg).

◼ CRYPTS

The vast crypts contain statues of saints and relics—including, it is said, the **Sacred Heart of Jesus**—from all over France. A stone urn in one of the crypts contains the **heart of Alexandre Legentil,** one of two Catholic businessmen (the other was Hubert Rohault de Fleury) whose idea it was to build this church dedicated to the Sacred Heart, a symbol of a loving Christ.

MONTMARTRE

Parvis du Sacré-Coeur, 18th arr. • tel 01 53 41 89 00 • Open every day 6 a.m.–10:30 p.m. • Dome and crypt: € • Métro: Abbesses or Anvers (then the funicular railway from Funiculaire Gare Basse; you can use a standard métro ticket) • sacre-coeur-montmartre.com

Cabarets

The reputation of Paris as a city of stylishly sexy nightlife dates from the pleasure-loving period of the late 19th century that the French call the *belle époque,* when Montmartre's cabarets were a mix of music hall, circus, strip clubs, and clip joints. They existed in a world of semi-legality, closely linked to the city's flourishing brothels, and attracted a rowdy working-class crowd alongside scions of wealthy families and bohemian artists.

Jane Avril (above) became one of Paris's best loved dancers with her graceful interpretation of the can-can that she performed at halls such as the Moulin Rouge (right)—considered the dance's spiritual home.

Erotic Art

The original cabaret performances relied on raucous energy and the exposure of female flesh. The songs were coarse and satirical, the dances uninhibitedly vulgar, including the famous can-can, which dancers often performed without underwear. But subtler artistic ambitions soon developed as the cabarets drifted upscale. In the 1890s, American dancer Loie Fuller established herself as the star of the Folies Bergère with an art nouveau-influenced act combining innovative lighting and an expressive form of free dance.

By the 1920s, **Casino de Paris** (*16 rue de Clichy, 9th arr., tel 08 92 69 89 26, casinodeparis.fr*) was showcasing the era's stars, including singer Maurice Chevalier and his partner Mistinguett. Meanwhile, the **Folies Bergère** (*32 rue Richer, 9th arr., tel 08 92 68 16 50, foliesbergere.com*) embraced jazz and found a new sensation in Josephine Baker, the African-American star, who catered for the Parisian taste in eroticism by dancing dressed only in a skirt made of bananas strung together.

Contemporary Cabaret

Over time, the successful cabarets lost contact with their popular roots. The **Moulin Rouge** (*82 blvd. de Clichy, 18th arr., tel 01 53 09 82 82, moulinrouge.fr*), for example, mutated into a slick entertainment venue for wealthy Parisians and tourists. But amid the upheaval of the 1968 student revolt, the cabaret tradition found a new lease on life when a group of young performers founded the self-proclaimed "ugly and dirty" **Café de la Gare** (*41 rue du Temple, 4th arr., tel 01 42 78 52 51, cdlg.org*) in an abandoned factory. As well as providing a springboard for a host of talents, including the young actor Gérard Depardieu, it spawned a new generation of "alternative" café-theaters that flourish in Paris today.

CABARET **THEATERS**

Olympia Restored to its belle époque splendor in the 1990s, Olympia, near La Madeleine, is now a major concert venue. **28 blvd. des Capucines, 9th arr., tel 08 92 68 33 68, olympiahall.com**

Le Point Virgule This theater is renowned for its offbeat stand-up comedy. **7 rue Ste.-Croix de la Bretonnerie, 4th arr., tel 01 42 78 67 03, lepointvirgule.com**

Le Zèbre de Belleville This Belleville venue offers zany contemporary dance and acrobatic routines. **63 blvd. de Belleville, 11th arr., tel 01 43 55 55 55, lezebre.com**

MONTMARTRE

Parisian Views

From the heights of the Tour Eiffel to the Basilique du Sacré-Coeur, several of Paris's buildings offer spectacular views. As in most major cities, vantage points range from landmarks known the world over to obscure panoramas where your fellow viewers are likely to be locals.

MONTMARTRE

■ BASILIQUE DU SACRÉ-COEUR
Montmartre's imposing basilica (see pp. 168–169) sits on Paris's tallest hill, giving excellent views across the sprawling city. Many people are content to gaze down from the terrace in front of the church, rather than climb the 300 steps to the top of the dome. From the terrace you get a great view of **St.-Vincent de Paul**'s green roof and towers, **Centre Pompidou**'s distinctive silhouette, and **Notre-Dame**'s imposing towers.

■ PARC DES BUTTES-CHAUMONT
In the 19th arrondisement, to the east of Montmartre, is a lesser-known vantage point in one of Paris's most beautiful parks *(rue Botzaris, 19th arr.)*, created by Baron Haussmann. The rugged topography of this onetime quarry and execution site culminates in the lookout point set on a cliff top and reached by means of a suspension bridge across a rocky gully. From here you have wonderful views across the city—it is an especially good vantage point for appreciating **Sacré-Coeur**'s white facade and dome.

■ INSTITUT DU MONDE ARABE
Until the moment when we can once again admire Paris from the top of Notre-Dame's northern tower, we can console ourselves with the view from the terrace on the ninth floor of the Institut du Monde Arabe (see p. 63) that encompasses **Notre-Dame** itself, **the Seine**, **Le Marais**, the **Île de la Cité** and the **Mémorial des Martyrs de la Déportation**.

■ TOUR MONTPARNASSE
The view from this 690-foot-high (210 m) tower (see p. 77) in the south of Montparnasse has the benefit of being the only place in Paris where you can't see the tower itself. It's a

See all of Paris laid out at your feet from the top of the Tour Eiffel.

great place for gazing down on **Les Invalides** and has a wonderful view of the **Tour Eiffel.**

■ Arc de Triomphe

Atop this 162-foot-high (49 m) arch (see pp. 138–139), which anchors one end of the **Champs-Élysées**, you'll have an excellent view of Paris's foremost boulevard and the other 11 streets that fan out from here. As you look east, the **Palais du Louvre** is at the far end of the Champs-Élysées, while looking west you can't miss the tower blocks of **La Défense.** The Arc de Triomphe is also a great place to watch the madness that is Parisian traffic, with its never-ending streams of cars, bikes, and buses jockeying and scrambling for position.

■ Tour Eiffel

The third deck of the 1,063-foot-tall (324 m) tower (see p. 149) offers, on a clear day, an outstanding panorama stretching 40 miles (64 km) to the French countryside. Yet the best views are from the second deck, with its bird's-eye take on Parisian life. Be sure to look north past the elegant gardens of the **Trocadéro** to the high-rise buildings of **La Défense** district.

PART 3

Travel Essentials

PLANNING YOUR TRIP

When to Go

In **August** many stores, restaurants, and private museums are closed, yet the city has less traffic and pollution and offers free activities such as *Paris Plages* (beaches on the Seine River), concerts in the parks, and outdoor movies at La Villette.

In **fall**, the weather is good, and the city bustles again. The **Christmas holidays** can light up the city.

Climate

Paris has moderately cold winters, cool springs and falls, and warm, humid summers.

Insurance

Travel with adequate cover for medical treatment and expenses; and also for repatriation, and baggage and money loss.

Passports & Visas

For U.S. and Canadian citizens, only a passport is needed to enter France for a stay of up to 90 days. No visa is required.

HOW TO GET TO PARIS

Airports

Paris has two airports: The larger **Roissy–Charles de Gaulle**, 19 miles (30 km) north of Paris, and **Orly**, 9 miles (15 km) south of Paris *(both: tel 39 50, or 01 70 36 39 50 from abroad; aeroportsdeparis.fr).*

From the Airports

Roissy–Charles de Gaulle has two main terminals—CDG1 and CDG2. **Le Bus Direct** *(tel 08 64 02 50 14, €18, lebusdirect.com)* operate routes to Porte Maillot, Étoile and Tour Eiffel every 30 minutes, taking 45 to 70 minutes; or to Gare Montparnasse and Gare de Lyon every 30 minutes, taking 40 to 80 minutes. The **RoissyBus** *(tel 34 24, €12.50, ratp.fr)* departs every 15 minutes and takes around 60 minutes to reach Opéra. For trains, the **RER Line B** *(tel 34 24, €10, ratp.fr)* leaves every 5 to 15 minutes and takes around 40 minutes to Gare du Nord. A taxi costs around €50 and takes up to 45 minutes to reach central Paris.

From Orly, the **Orlybus** *(tel 34 24, €8.70, ratp.fr)* departs every 20 minutes and takes 30 minutes to reach Denfert-Rochereau. **Le Bus Direct** *(tel 08 64 02 50 14, €18, lebusdirect.com)* departs every 20 minutes, stops at Gare Montparnasse, Trocadéro, and Étoile, takes around 30 minutes to reach the city center, and costs €12. The **Orlyval train** connects with RER at Antony station, from where a connecting train goes to Châtelet – Les Halles. A taxi costs around €30 and takes up to 45 minutes.

Although expensive, you can also arrange for a door-to-door shuttle: **Super Shuttle Paris** *(tel 01 41 47 13 13, supershuttle.fr).*

GETTING AROUND

Mass Transit

Paris's bus, métro, and suburban rail (RER) service is operated by RATP *(tel 34 24, ratp.fr).* Métro and rail services run from 5:30 a.m. to 1 a.m. (2 a.m. Fri.–Sat.).

Buses

A map of bus lines is posted at bus shelters. Some lines do not operate after 8:30 p.m., or on Sundays and holidays. Late night bus lines, called **Noctilien**, leave from Châtelet, Montparnasse, Gare de l'Est, Gare St.-Lazare, and Gare de Lyon. The **Batobus** *(batobus.com)* river buses run between the Tour Eiffel and the Jardin des Plantes.

Métro tickets can be used on city buses (validate one-use tickets in the machine behind the driver) or tickets can be purchased from the driver (exact change not required).

Métro

Each **métro** line has a number, and is identified by the names of the stations at either end: The east–west Line 1, for example, is La Défense–Château de Vincennes.

Individual tickets cost €1.90, but a *carnet* (book) of **ten tickets** costs €14.90. If you plan to travel extensively, the **Passe Navigo Découverte** is good for unlimited trips on the métro, RER, and buses for one month or one week. You will need a passport-size photo for the pass. A **Paris Visite** card is good for one, two, three, or five days and entitles you to unlimited use of public transportation in

Paris and discounts at some sightseeing attractions. The **Mobilis** card is good for one day of transport.

Do not throw away a one-use ticket until you have left the station; a *contrôleur* (conductor) may ask to see your ticket and will fine you if you don't have it.

RER

The suburban train network has stops in Paris, and you can use a métro ticket to travel on it within Paris. Prices are higher for destinations outside the city.

Trains

The national French railroad, the **SNCF** *(tel 36 35 for information, 09 80 98 36 35 for bookings; sncf.com)* links all major cities. Buy your ticket online or at the station—the phone service is expensive.

The Paris mainline SNCF train stations (each with a métro station of the same name) are the **Gare de Lyon** (for traveling to/from the southeast of France and/to Italy); the **Gare du Nord** (Brussels, London, and other northern destinations); the **Gare de l'Est** (the east); the **Gare St.-Lazare** (the northwest, including Normandy); the **Gare d'Austerlitz** (Spain and the southwest); and the **Gare Montparnasse** (the west, including Brittany).

The high-speed *Train à Grande Vitesse* **(TGV)** will get you to Marseilles in around three hours, Zürich in four and a half hours, Luxembourg in two hours, or Brussels in an hour and a half; reserve in advance.

Before boarding any train, *composter* (validate) your ticket in one of the yellow machines at the start of each journey. You may be fined if you don't.

Taxis

Taxis can be hailed on the street or found at a *station de taxi* (taxi stand) at major intersections. When the entire light on top is glowing, the taxi is available, but if only the small bulb is lit, it is not. Some new cabs have green/red lights to indicate availability. Extra charges are added for pickups at train stations, heavy luggage, a fourth passenger, and an animal (except a seeing-eye dog).

If you call for a taxi, the meter starts running when the driver receives the call, and the fare can be expensive. Ask for a receipt in case you leave something behind, or have a problem with the driver. Fares go up at night and when the cab passes the city limits. Complaints should be addressed to Service des Taxis, Préfecture de Police *(36 rue des Morillons, 15th arr., tel 01 55 76 20 05).*

Radio-Dispatched Taxis
Taxis G7, *tel 36 07, g7.fr*

Tours
Bicycle
City Segway Tours, *tel 01 85 08 19 76, for bookings 01 82 88 80 96 or (North America toll free) 01 866 614 6218, citysegwaytours.com/paris*
Paris à Vélo C'est Sympa, *tel 01 48 87 60 01, parisvelosympa.com*

Boat
The following companies offer regular Seine tours, starting at around 10 a.m. and ending between 10 p.m. and 11 p.m.
Bateaux-Mouches, *tel 01 42 25 96 10, bateaux-mouches.fr*
Bateaux Parisiens Tour Eiffel, *tel 08 25 01 01 01, bateauxparisiens.com*
Bateaux Vedettes du Pont Neuf, *tel 01 46 33 98 38, vedettesdupontneuf.com*

Bus
BigBus Paris, *tel 01 53 953 953, bigbustours.com*
Paris Open Tour, *tel 01 42 66 56 56, paris.opentour.com*

Walking
Fat Tire Tours, tel *01 82 88 80 96, fattiretours.com/paris/tours/the-classic-walking-tour*
Paris Walks, *tel 01 48 09 21 40, paris-walks.com*

PRACTICAL ADVICE

Electricity
French circuits use 220 volts; a transformer and adapter plug are needed for American appliances that operate on 110 volts. Ask for one at a *droguerie* (hardware store), such as the basement of BHV *(52 rue de Rivoli, 1st arr.)*, at the airport, or before you leave home.

Local Customs
Say *"bonjour"* and *"au revoir"* to the staff when entering and leaving a shop, restaurant, or café. The French tend to

keep to themselves more than Americans do, but as elsewhere a friendly approach usually gets a friendly response, and certainly the locals are always more than willing to give directions. If you are invited to dinner at a French person's home, bring flowers rather than wine.

Money Matters

American Express, *11 rue Scribe, 2nd arr., tel 01 47 77 70 00 or 01 47 77 72 00*
Banque de France, *31 rue Croix-des-Petits-Champs, 1st arr., tel 01 42 92 42 92*

One euro equals 100 cents, which come in coins of 1, 2, 5, 10, 20, and 50. The euro comes in coins of 1 and 2, and bills of 5, 10, 20, 50, 100, 200, and 500, although shops may not accept bills over 50.

ATMs are the easiest way to get money, but check with your bank before leaving. A fee may be charged.

Commercial currency exchanges are located in train stations, airports, and numerous locations around the city. Bank branches that exchange currency display a sign saying *"Change."* A commission is usually charged.

National Holidays

January 1, Easter Monday, May 1, May 8, Ascension (40 days after Easter), Pentecost Monday (10 days after Ascension), July 14, August 15, November 1, November 11, December 25.

Opening Times

Most **banks** are open Monday to Friday, from 9 a.m. to 5 p.m. Some close at lunchtime or open on Saturday morning. Major **department stores** are open from about 9:30 a.m. to 7 p.m., and some stay open until 10 p.m. one night a week. **Boutiques** open around 10 a.m. and close at 7 or 8 p.m.; they may be closed on Monday and at lunchtime, usually between 1 p.m. and 2:30 p.m. More and more shops are staying open on Sunday, but check first. **Cafés** are open from early morning until 8 p.m., 10 p.m., or 2 a.m. Most **restaurants** are open from 12 noon to 3 p.m. and 7:30 p.m. to 11 p.m. Many stores and restaurants close in August.

Postal Service

Due to work, the main post office branch (*52 rue du Louvre, 1st arr., tel 36 31, laposte.fr*) has been temporarily transferred to rue Étienne Marcel 16. Local branches are open Monday to Friday 8 a.m. to 7 or 8 p.m.; Saturday 8 or 9 a.m. to 12 noon or 1 p.m.

The French postal service has branches in every neighborhood. All Paris postal codes begin with 75 and end with the number of the arrondissement, or quarter. For example, 75010 is in the 10th arrondissement, 75002 in the 2nd arrondissement, and so on.

Yellow *boîtes postales* (mailboxes) may have separate compartments for local mail, *départemental* (mail within the *département*), and *autres*

départements/étranger (elsewhere in France and foreign).

Restrooms

The self-cleaning toilets on the street (now wheelchair-accessible) are free, and should not be used by children under ten unless accompanied by an adult. Some métro stations and large department stores have public restrooms.

Telephones

To call France from the U.S., dial 011-33 (international and French country code) and the nine-digit number (leaving out the initial zero).

To make a domestic call from a telephone booth, buy a *télécarte* (phonecard) in a post office or *tabac* (tobacco shop). The following instructions will appear on the telephone's screen: *"décrochez"* (pick up the receiver); *"insérez votre carte"* (insert your card); *"patientez"* (wait); *"numérotez/composez"* (dial); and *"raccrochez"* (hang up).

French phone numbers have ten digits, with Paris-region numbers beginning with 01. Numbers beginning with 08 00 are toll free, and there is an extra charge for other numbers beginning with 08. For directory assistance, dial 118 712 or go to *pagesjaunes.fr/pagesblanches* (individuals) or *pagesjaunes.fr* (businesses).

Time Differences

If it is 12 midnight in Paris, it is 6 p.m. in New York and 3 p.m. in California. Europe changes to daylight saving time (when clocks move forward one hour) on the last Sunday of March and returns to standard time on the last Sunday in October. However, this practice may be abolished by fall 2021.

Tipping

All restaurant bills include a 15 percent service charge. It is usual to leave a small additional tip for the waiter. It is customary to tip taxi drivers 10 percent, though this is not obligatory. It is usual to give porters and doormen a tip of €1 to €2, and ushers and cloakroom attendants 50 cents.

Tourist Offices

In the U.S.
New York, tel 212/838-7800

Office de Tourisme de Paris
29 rue de Rivoli, 4th arr., tel 01 49 52 42 63, parisinfo.com. Open daily 9 a.m.–7 p.m, Nov.–Apr. from 10 a.m. Staff will answer questions and help with hotel reservations. There are branches at airports and train stations.

Travelers with Disabilities

The new Météor métro line is wheelchair accessible. **Taxis G7** *(tel 01 47 39 00 91, staffed 24/7)* provides a service called Horizon, dedicated to people with limited mobility, or request a **Renault-Espace** taxi from any taxi service. Persons with disabilities do not have to wait in line for a taxi at an airport or train station.

Access to the métro is nearly impossible for anyone

in a wheelchair, and only a few RER stations are easily accessible. Cité Universitaire, Auber, and Charles de Gaulle – Étoile have public elevators. At the following stations, you must ask a station employee to accompany you as the elevators require a key: Châtelet – Les Halles, Gare de Lyon, Grande Arche de la Défense, Denfert – Rochereau, St.-Michel Notre-Dame, Porte de Clichy, Porte Maillot, Avenue Foch, Avenue Henri-Martin, Boulainvilliers, Avenue du Président Kennedy, and Invalides. Other stations are not accessible. Of the **bus lines,** only Line 20 (Gare St.-Lazare–Gare de Lyon) is wheelchair accessible. Spaces are reserved for wheelchairs in the high-speed TGV trains, and there are accessible toilets.

Most **hotel** elevators are too small for a wheelchair, and bathrooms can be tiny. Modern hotels are the most likely to be accessible. There is a ramp at the curb on every street corner. **RADAR** puts out *Access in Paris,* an English-language guide for disabled travelers (*accessinparis. org*). The Paris Tourist Office has information on the accessibility of transportation, museums, and monuments. Pamphlets on train and métro accessibility are available at all stations. Always clearly describe your needs when booking any travel service.

Escort Services for Travelers with Disabilities
Auxiliaires des Aveugles, *71 ave. de Breteuil, 15th arr., tel 01 88 32 31 40, lesauxiliairesdesaveugles.asso.fr.*

Free escorts for the visually impaired.

EMERGENCIES

Embassies & Consulates
United States Embassy, *2 ave. Gabriel, 8th arr., tel 01 43 12 22 22, fr.usembassy.gov*
Canadian Embassy, *130, rue du Faubourg Saint-Honoré, 8th arr., tel 01 44 43 29 00, canadainternational.gc.ca/france*

Emergency Phone Numbers
Any emergency *tel 112*
Police *tel 17*
Fire or **emergency medical assistance** *tel 18*
Ambulance *tel 15* or *01 44 49 23 23*
American Hospital *63 blvd. de Victor-Hugo, Neuilly, 17th arr., tel 01 46 41 25 25.* For 24-hour bilingual emergency medical and dental services.
Dental emergencies *tel 01 42 61 12 00.* Emergency dental service from 8 a.m. to 10 p.m. Sunday and holidays.
24-hour pharmacy, Pharmacie les Champs-Élysées, *84 ave. des Champs-Élysées, 8th arr., tel 01 45 62 02 41*
SOS Help *tel 01 46 21 46 46.* English-language crisis hotline, 3 p.m. to 11 p.m.

Lost Property
Bureau des Objets Trouvés (Lost and Found) *36 rue des Morillons, 15th arr, tel 08 21 00 25 25. Open: Mon.–Thurs. 8:30 a.m.– 5 p.m., Fri. 8:30 a.m.–4:30 p.m.*
RATP Lost and Found *tel 32 46*

HOTELS

Paris is home to some of the world's finest hotels. With more than a thousand places to stay, every type of lodging can be found here, from opulent *palaces* (luxury hotels) to simple, family-friendly hotels and small romantic residences. When choosing a hotel, decide on a location, and then find a place that suits your plans and budget. The Parisian hotels here are listed by location, price, and then in alphabetical order. Unless otherwise mentioned, all these hotels have private bathrooms with shower and/or bathtub. Value-added tax and service are included in the prices, but a hotel tax per person per night will be added to the bill.

TRAVEL ESSENTIALS

Although bargains can be found, Paris hotels are some of the most expensive in the world—the average room costs around €200. The best deals can be found by booking well in advance, and many hotels have offers on their websites. It may also be worth calling to ask a hotel for their "best price." Most places now charge extra for breakfast, usually continental style (bread, croissant, jam, and tea or coffee), but sometimes buffet style. Yet with so much to do in a city famous for its café culture, you may prefer to eat breakfast out.

Street parking is extremely difficult to find in Paris, and most hotels do not have parking lots or garages.

Little has been done to make the city's hotels accessible to the disabled. "Accessible Room" means that a wheelchair would be able to get into a room and move around, and "adapted" means that the bathroom is up to standards. However, there are no specific facilities for the disabled, and buildings may have steps to navigate before entering. Travelers with disabilities should check when booking to make sure the hotel meets their needs.

If your hotel is on a main street, ask for a room at the back where you will not be disturbed by traffic.

Price Range
An indication of the cost of a double room in the high season is given by € signs.

€€€€€	Over €300
€€€€	€220–€300
€€€	€150–€220
€€	€100–€150
€	Under €100

Text Symbols
- 🛏 *No. of Guest Rooms & Suites*
- 🚇 *Métro*
- ⬆ *Elevator*
- ❄ *Air-conditioning*
- 🚭 *Non-smoking*
- 🅿 *Parking*
- 🏋 *Health Club*
- 🏊 *Indoor Pool*
- 🕐 *Closed*
- 💳 *Credit Cards*

THE ISLANDS
The Île de la Cité and the Île St.-Louis have a few charming hotels in the heart of Paris.

■ Des Deux Îles
€€€
59 RUE ST.-LOUIS-EN-L'ÎLE, 4TH ARR.
TEL 01 43 26 13 35
deuxiles-paris-hotel.com
Located on the chic Île St.-Louis. Small, attractive rooms, some with exposed wooden beams.
🛏 17 🚇 *Pont Marie* ⬆ ❄ 💳 AE, MC, V

■ De Lutèce
€€€
65 RUE ST.-LOUIS-EN-L'ÎLE, 4TH ARR.
TEL 01 43 26 23 52
paris-hotel-lutece.com
A fire burns in the lobby's fireplace, and modest rooms have antique furniture or vintage tiles.
🛏 23 ❄ 🚇 *Pont Marie* ⬆ 💳 AE, MC, V

■ Du Jeu de Paume
€€€
54 RUE ST.-LOUIS-EN-L'ÎLE, 4TH ARR.
TEL 01 43 26 14 18
jeudepaumehotel.com
A 17th-century tennis court

converted into a hotel. Rooms are comfortable, but small.

(i) 30 🚇 Pont Marie 🔁 📶 🔷 All major cards

QUARTIER LATIN

Small hotels are the rule in the famous student quarter, which has many cheap restaurants.

■ Des Grands Hommes
€€€€€
17 PLACE DU PANTHÉON, 5TH ARR.
TEL 01 46 34 19 60
hoteldesgrandshommes.com
This pretty hotel is decorated in Empire style. Ask for one of the attic rooms that have a view of the Panthéon across the street. Some of the rooms have canopy beds.

(i) 31 🚇 Maubert-Mutualité, RER: Luxembourg 🔁 📶 🔷 All major cards

■ Le Clos Médicis
€€€
56 RUE MONSIEUR-LE-PRINCE, 6TH ARR.
TEL 01 43 29 10 80
closmedicis.com
Designer furnishings meet stone walls and exposed beams in this mid-18th-century hotel. Small but comfortable rooms.

(i) 38 🚇 Odéon, RER: Luxembourg 🔁 📶 🔷 All major cards

■ Le Petit Paris
€€€
214 RUE ST. JACQUES, 5TH ARR.
TEL 01 53 10 29 29
hotelpetitparis.com
A historic 16th-century inn turned into a boutique hotel in a convenient location close

to both the Panthéon and the Luxembourg Gardens.

(i) 20 🚇 Luxembourg, RER 🔁 📶 🔷 📶 All major cards

■ Parc St.-Séverin
€€€
22 RUE DE LA PARCHEMINERIE, 5TH ARR.
TEL 01 43 54 32 17
FAX 01 43 54 70 71
paris-hotel-parcsaintseverin.com
An attractive hotel with a mix of modern and antique furnishings on a quiet street. Bright, spacious rooms, some of which have pleasant rooftop terraces.

(i) 27 🚇 St.-Michel, Cluny La Sorbonne 🔁 📶 🔷 All major cards

■ The Five Hotel
€€
3 RUE FLATTERS, 5TH ARR.
TEL 01 43 31 74 21
thefivehotel.com
Ultra-modern hotel in the Latin Quarter, with themed rooms. For romance, book the all-red Love Capsule room.

🚇 Les Gobelins 🔁 📶 📶 🔷 All major cards

ST.-GERMAIN & MONTPARNASSE

The chic neighborhood of St.-Germain-des-Prés has many charming hotels, some of them quite reasonably priced, as well as many interesting little restaurants. Montparnasse is more modest, but it has plenty of points of interest.

■ De l'Odéon St.-Germain
€€€€€
13 RUE ST.-SULPICE, 6TH ARR.
TEL 01 43 25 70 11
paris-hotel-odeon.com
Antiques and tapestries in this 16th-century manor house create a romantic setting.

(i) 27 🚇 Odéon 🔁 📶 🔷 All major cards

■ L'Hôtel St.-Germain
€€€€€
13 RUE DES BEAUX-ARTS, 6TH ARR.
TEL 01 44 41 99 00
l-hotel.com
This hotel has a marvelous round stairway and extravagantly decorated rooms. Oscar Wilde died in room 16.

(i) 20 🚇 St.-Germain-des-Prés 🔁 📶 🔷 All major cards

■ Recamier
€€€€€
3 BIS PLACE ST.-SULPICE, 6TH ARR.
TEL 01 43 26 04 89
www.hotelrecamier.com
This small gem of a hotel has tastefully decorated rooms and faces Saint-Sulpice square.

(i) 24 🚇 St.-Sulpice 🔁 📶 📶 🔷 All major cards

■ Relais Christine St.-Germaine
€€€€€
3 RUE CHRISTINE, 6TH ARR.
TEL 01 40 51 60 80
FAX 01 40 51 60 81
relais-christine.com
Discreet, Left Bank luxury in a former convent, in whose vaulted, 13th-century

kitchens breakfast is served. Garden and courtyard.

51 Odéon, St.-Michel
All major cards

■ **D'Angleterre St.-Germain**
€€€€
44 RUE JACOB, 6TH ARR.
TEL 01 42 60 34 72
hotel-dangleterre.com
Historical associations (Washington Irving and Ernest Hemingway stayed here) and plenty of charm in individually decorated rooms.

26 St.-Germain-des-Prés
All major cards

■ **Esprit Saint Germain**
€€€€
22 RUE ST.-SULPICE, 6TH ARR.
TEL 01 53 10 55 55
FAX 01 53 10 55 56
hotel-esprit-saint-germain.com
An intimate, award-winning boutique hotel close to St.-Sulpice Church, with luxuriously decorated rooms and great service.

28 St.-Sulpice
All major cards

■ **De l'Abbaye St-Germain**
€€€
10 RUE CASSETTE, 6TH ARR.
TEL 01 45 44 38 11
hotelabbayeparis.com
Charming 18th-century building with a courtyard garden on a quiet street. Four duplex suites with terraces. Some rooms are quite small.

44 St.-Sulpice
AE, MC, V

■ **Des Sts.-Pères St.-Germain**
€€€
65 RUE DES STS.-PÈRES, 6TH ARR.
TEL 01 45 44 50 00
FAX 01 45 44 90 83
paris-hotel-saints-peres.com
Beloved of the fashion crowd, most of its antique-furnished rooms have views of the garden. The lounge bar is popular with writers.

39 St.-Germain-des-Prés
AE, MC, V

■ **Istria St.-Germain**
€€€
29 RUE CAMPAGNE-PREMIÈRE, 14TH ARR.
TEL 01 43 20 91 82
hotel-istria-paris.com
A well-kept hotel on a quiet street; its past guests have included French artist Marcel Duchamp and American photographer Man Ray.

26 Raspail
All major cards

■ **Left Bank St.-Germain Best Western**
€€€–€€€€€
9 RUE DE L'ANCIENNE COMÉDIE, 6TH ARR.
TEL 01 43 54 01 70
FAX 01 43 26 17 14
hotelleftbank.com
This small hotel has an antique-filled lobby, wooden beams, and marble bathrooms. Some rooms open onto inside gardens.

31 Odéon
All major cards

■ **Odéon-Hôtel St.-Germain**
€€€
3 RUE DE L'ODÉON, 6TH ARR.
TEL 01 43 25 90 67
FAX 01 43 25 55 98

odeonhotel.fr
A quiet, central location between Boulevard St.-Germain and the popular Jardin du Luxembourg.

33 Odéon
All major cards

■ **Pullman Paris Montparnasse**
€€€
19 RUE COMMANDANT RENÉ MOUCHOTTE, 14TH ARR.
TEL 01 44 36 44 36
FAX 01 44 36 47 00
pullman.accorhotels.com
Reopening in May 2020, a modern, high-rise hotel with business facilities and good views from the upper floors. Choice of two restaurants.

953 Montparnasse–Bienvenüe
All major cards

■ **De Nesle**
€€–€€€
7 RUE DE NESLE, 6TH ARR.
TEL 01 43 54 62 41
hoteldenesleparis.com
Close to place de L'Odéon, this rustic hotel is a great buy. Check out the second-floor garden.

21 Odéon
All major cards

CHÂTELET & LES HALLES
The heart of the city is noisy and congested, but the hotels listed below are on relatively quiet streets.

■ **Le Relais des Halles**
€€€€
26 RUE PIERRE LESCOT, 1ST. ARR.
TEL 01 44 82 64 00
hotel-relais-des-halles.com

Centrally located near the Pompidou and the Louvre, this small hotel has typical French furnishings with soundproofed rooms.

(i) 19 **🚇** *Étienne Marcel* **⇄** 🆒
🆒 *All major cards*

■ Britannique
€€€
20 AVE. VICTORIA, 1ST ARR.
TEL 01 42 33 74 59
FAX 01 42 33 82 65
hotel-britannique.fr
Cozy, British-influenced comfort on a quiet street in the busy city center. Charming, beautiful rooms, with helpful staff.

(i) 40 **🚇** *Châtelet* **⇄** 🆒
🆒 *All major cards*

■ Hôtel Le Presbytère
€€€
78 RUE DE LA VERRERIE, 4TH ARR.
TEL 01 42 78 14 15
FAX 01 40 29 06 82
hotel-le-presbytere.com
This used to be a presbytery of the St.-Merri Church, whose flying buttresses form part of the decor of Room 9. Expensive rooms have authentic, carved-wood Gothic furnishings; cheaper ones might not have private bathrooms, but they do have showers, and are charmingly decorated with matching wallpaper, bedspreads, and curtains.

(i) 12 **🚇** *Hôtel de Ville* 🆒 *AE, MC, V*

LE MARAIS & BASTILLE

The Marais does not have many hotels, but there are a few interesting options, as well as good restaurants. The Bastille area is moving upscale, thanks to the Opera House, but it may not be the most desirable area to stay.

■ Pavillon de la Reine
€€€€€
28 PLACE DES VOSGES, 3RD ARR.
TEL 01 40 29 19 19
FAX 01 40 29 19 20
pavillon-de-la-reine.com
Antique-furnished rooms, some with four-poster beds, make this an extremely romantic hotel. The garden is peaceful.

(i) 56 **🚇** *St.-Paul* **⇄** 🆒 🆒 *All major cards*

■ Hôtel Jeanne d'Arc
€€€€
3 RUE DE JARENTE, 4TH ARR.
TEL 01 48 87 62 11
hoteljeannedarc.com
A fine little hotel, much in demand because of its central location and good value for money. Rooms are simple yet pleasant, individually decorated, and include modern conveniences.

(i) 35 **🚇** *St.-Paul* **⇄** 🆒 *MC, V*

■ Caron de Beaumarchais
€€€
12 RUE VIEILLE-DU-TEMPLE, 4TH ARR.
TEL 01 42 72 34 12
carondebeaumarchais.com
The 18th century is brought back to life in this pretty hotel.

(i) 19 **🚇** *St.-Paul, Hôtel de Ville* **⇄** 🆒 🆒 *AE, MC, V*

■ De la Bretonnerie
€€
22 RUE STE.-CROIX DE LA

BRETONNERIE, 4TH. ARR.
TEL 01 48 87 77 63
FAX 01 42 77 26 78
hotelparismaraisbretonnerie.com
Brittany-style hotel with beam ceilings and canopy beds in a former 17th-century mansion.

(i) 29 **🚇** *Hôtel de Ville* **⇄** 🆒
🆒 *All major cards*

■ De Nice
€€–€€€€
42 BIS, RUE DE RIVOLI, 4TH ARR.
TEL 01 42 78 55 29
FAX 01 42 78 36 07
hoteldenice.com
Antique furnishings and a central location at reasonable prices.

(i) 23 **🚇** *Hôtel de Ville* **⇄**
🆒 *MC, V*

■ Émile
€€
2 RUE MAHLER, 4TH ARR.
TEL 01 42 72 76 17
hotelemile.com
Renovated hotel in the heart of the Marais with views of historic St.-Paul Church.

(i) 29 **🚇** *St.-Paul* 🆒 🆒
🆒 *All major cards*

THE LOUVRE & PALAIS-ROYAL

A few grand hotels can be found in this palatial neighborhood, close to many of the city's best known museums, palaces, monuments, and some great restaurants.

■ Du Louvre
€€€€
1 PLACE ANDRÉ MALRAUX, 1ST ARR.
TEL 01 73 11 12 34
FAX 01 73 11 13 34
hoteldulouvre.com

Pissarro painted the view from his window in this luxury hotel. The Opera House can be viewed from Room 551's bath.

ⓘ 177 🏨 *Palais-Royal, Musée du Louvre* 🔁 🔄 ♿ *All major cards*

■ Konfidentiel Paris
€€€€
64 RUE DE L'ARBRE SEC, 1ST ARR.
TEL 01 55 34 40 40
konfidentiel-paris.com
A fun hotel near the Louvre, whose themed rooms have names such as Marie-Antoinette and King of France.

ⓘ 15 🏨 *Louvre-Rivoli, Pont Neuf* 🔁 🔄 🅿 ♿ *All major cards*

■ The Westin Paris
€€€€
3 RUE CASTIGLIONE, 1ST ARR.
TEL 01 44 77 11 11
FAX 01 44 77 14 60
thewestinparis.com
The century-old splendor of this hotel has been refurbished. Two restaurants, spa.

ⓘ 450 🏨 *Concorde, Tuileries* 🔁 🔄 📺 ♿ *All major cards*

■ Thérèse
€€€€
5–7 RUE DE THÉRÈSE, 1ST ARR.
TEL 01 42 96 10 01
hoteltherese.com
A designer boutique hotel near the Palais-Royal and rue Saint-Honoré.

ⓘ 40 🏨 *Palais-Royal* 🔁 🔄 🔄 ♿ *All major cards*

■ De la Place du Louvre
€€€
21 RUE DES PRÊTRES-ST.-GERMAIN-L'AUXERROIS, 1ST ARR.
TEL 01 42 33 78 68
FAX 01 42 33 09 95

paris-hotel-place-du-louvre .com
Facing the Louvre. Breakfast is served in a cave that was once connected to the Louvre.

ⓘ 20 🏨 *Louvre-Rivoli, Pont Neuf* 🔁 🔄 ♿ *All major cards*

CHAMPS-ÉLYSÉES
Most of the city's top hotels are located in the Champs-Élysées' environs.

■ Balzac
€€€€€
6 RUE BALZAC, 8TH ARR.
TEL 01 44 35 18 00
hotelbalzac.com
Luxurious, elegant, belle époque building with huge rooms. The restaurant is the home of the great chef Pierre Gagnaire.

ⓘ 79 🏨 *George V* 🔁 🔄 ♿ *All major cards*

■ Castille
€€€€€
33–37 RUE CAMBON, 1ST ARR.
TEL 01 44 58 44 58
FAX 01 44 58 44 00
castille.com
Venetian-style luxury near the Place Vendôme in a former annex of the Ritz. Italian restaurant with terrace.

ⓘ 108 🏨 *Concorde, Madeleine* 🅿 🔁 🔄 🔄 ♿ *All major cards*

■ Four Seasons Hotel George V
€€€€€
31 AVENUE GEORGE V, 8TH ARR.
TEL 01 49 52 70 00
fourseasons.com/paris
This venerable palace hotel with its fine antiques and tapestries reopened in 1999

after renovation. Courtyard garden and in-house restaurants.

ⓘ 245 🏨 *Alma-Marceau, George V,* 🔁 🔄 📺 🔄 ♿ *All major cards*

■ Mandarin Oriental Paris
€€€€€
251 RUE ST.-HONORÉ, 1ST ARR.
TEL 01 70 98 78 88
mandarinoriental.com/paris/ hotel
The Asian luxury chain delivers the five-star accommodation and service it is known for worldwide right near Place Vendôme. Celebrity chef Thierry Marx creates exquisite cuisine at the hotel's formal **Sur Mesure** and the more casual **Camélia** restaurants. The spa is one of the best in the city with a large indoor pool.

ⓘ 177 🏨 *Concorde* 🔁 🔄 🔄 🅿 📺 🔄 ♿ *All major cards*

■ Marignan Champs-Élysées
€€€€€
12 RUE MARIGNAN, 8TH ARR.
TEL 01 40 76 34 56
hotelmarignanelyseesparis.com
Antique furnishings, a Beauvais tapestry in the salon, and comfortable, simply decorated rooms. Tearoom.

ⓘ 73 🏨 *Franklin D. Roosevelt* 🔁 🔄 ♿ *All major cards*

■ Shangri-La Hotel Paris
€€€€€
10 AVE. D'IÉNA, 16TH ARR.
TEL 01 53 67 19 98
shangri-la.com/paris/shangrila
The former mansion of Prince Roland, the grandnephew of Napoleon Bonaparte, is the

ultimate in French-meets-Asian luxury. Indulge in a Cantonese feast at Michelin-starred **Shang Palace Restaurant.**
(i) *101* **(icon)** *léna* **(icon) (icon) (icon)**
(icon) (icon) (icon) *All major cards*

■ **The Peninsula Paris**
€€€€€
19 AVE. KLÉBER, 16TH ARR.
TEL 01 58 12 28 88
paris.peninsula.com
Steps from the Arc de Triomphe and the Champs-Élysées, this opulent palace hotel is where Henry Kissinger signed the Paris Peace Accord to end the Vietnam War in 1973. The rooftop restaurant **L'Oiseau Blanc** has breathtaking views of the Eiffel Tower and the city.
(i) *200* **(icon)** *Kleber* **(icon) (icon) (icon)**
(icon) (icon) (icon) (icon) *All major cards*

■ **Vernet**
€€€€€
25 RUE VERNET, 8TH ARR.
TEL 01 44 31 98 00
FAX 01 44 31 85 69
hotelvernet.com
A highly intimate, luxurious gem. The lobby has a fireplace and a piano. There are Jacuzzis in all the bathrooms and flatscreen televisions in the bedrooms. Gustave Eiffel designed the roof of the belle époque gourmet restaurant. There is also access to the Royal Monceau's luxury spa and pool.
(i) *51* **(icon)** *George V* **(icon) (icon) (icon)**
(icon) *AE, MC, V*

■ **Cambon**
€€€€
3 RUE CAMBON, 1ST ARR.
TEL 01 44 58 93 93
hotelcambonparis.com

Stylish, modern comfort near the Place de la Concorde. Each room is individually decorated. **(i)** *40* **(icon)** *Concorde*
(icon) (icon)
(icon) *All major cards*

■ **Le Pavillon des Lettres**
€€€€
12 RUE DES SAUSSAIES,
8TH ARR.
TEL 01 49 24 26 26
FAX 01 49 24 26 27
pavillondeslettres.com
A "literary" hotel run by Le Pavillon de la Reine, with each room devoted to a different writer or poet.
(i) *26* **(icon)** *Miromesnil* **(icon)**
(icon) *All major cards*

■ **Maison Astor Paris**
€€€€
11 RUE D'ASTORG, 8TH ARR.
TEL 01 53 05 05 05
maisonastorparis.com
Elegant Regency-revival decor on a quiet street. Some rooms have balconies or terraces. Gourmet restaurant.
(i) *128* **(icon)** *Champs-Élysées Clemenceau* **(icon) (icon) (icon) (icon)**
(icon) *All major cards*

■ **Renaissance Paris le Parc Trocadéro**
€€€€
55 AVENUE RAYMOND-POINCARÉ, 16TH ARR.
TEL 01 44 05 66 66
marriott.com
Elegant decor in this luxury hotel in five buildings, with a garden. Titular chef Xavier Pistol. Business facilities.
(i) *1122* **(icon)** *Trocadéro* **(icon) (icon)**
(icon) (icon) (icon) *All major cards*

■ **Galiléo**
€€€
54 RUE GALILÉE, 8TH ARR.
TEL 01 47 20 66 06
galileo-paris-hotel.com
The rooms are comfortable in this wonderfully refined small hotel.
(i) *27* **(icon)** *George V* **(icon) (icon)**
(icon) *AE, MC, V*

■ **Hotel Pergolèse**
€€
3 RUE PERGOLÈSE, 16TH ARR.
TEL 01 53 64 04 04
FAX 01 53 64 04 40
pergolese.com
Warm, modern rooms with designer decor and marble bathrooms. Bar.
(i) *40* **(icon)** *Argentine* **(icon) (icon) (icon)**
(icon) *All major cards*

TOUR EIFFEL & LES INVALIDES

A quiet, upper-class, residential area with some lovely hotels and fine eateries.

■ **Montalembert**
€€€€€
3 RUE MONTALEMBERT, 7TH ARR.
TEL 01 45 49 68 68
FAX 01 45 49 69 49
hotelmontalembert-paris.com
Fashionable hotel with designer lobby and attractive contemporary or traditional style rooms. Business facilities, **Le Montalembert** restaurant.
(i) *56* **(icon)** *Rue du Bac* **(icon) (icon)**
(icon) (icon) *All major cards*

■ **De l'Université**
€€€€
22 RUE DE L'UNIVERSITÉ, 7TH ARR.
TEL 01 42 61 09 39

hoteluniversite.com
Antique-furnished hotel with high attention to detail.
27 St.-Germain-des-Prés, Rue du Bac All major cards

■ Duc de St.-Simon
€€€€–€€€€€
14 RUE ST.-SIMON, 7TH ARR.
TEL 01 44 39 20 20
FAX 01 45 48 68 25
hotelducdesaintsimon.com
A luxurious haven on the Left Bank, with exquisite antique furnishings. The courtyard garden and breakfast room are both full of charm.
34 Rue du Bac
All major cards

■ Le Bellechasse
€€€€
8 RUE DE BELLECHASSE, 7TH ARR.
TEL 01 45 50 22 31
FAX 01 45 51 52 36
lebellechasse.com
A short walk from the Musée d'Orsay, with new designer decor and soundproof rooms.
34 Solférino
All major cards

■ Bersolys
€€€
28 RUE DE LILLE, 7TH ARR.
TEL 01 42 60 73 79, 01 42 60 19 05
FAX 09 56 61 21 47
bersolys-paris-hotel.com
A quiet hotel with small but attractive rooms.
16 Rue du Bac
Closed Aug. AE, MC, V

■ De l'Académie
€€€–€€€€€
32 RUE DES STS.-PÈRES,

7TH ARR.
TEL 01 45 49 80 00
FAX 01 45 44 75 24
academiehotel.com
A 17th-century building with period details such as exposed beams in the rooms.
33 St.-Germain-des-Prés
All major cards

■ Grand Hôtel Lévêque
€
29 RUE CLER, 7TH ARR.
TEL 01 47 05 49 15
hotel-leveque.com
Great location, with well-kept rooms at a good price.
50 École Militaire
All major cards

MONTMARTRE
Montmartre has a bohemian feel and a small number of attractive hotels if you don't mind being in a hilly location.

■ Particulier Montmartre
€€€€–€€€€€
23 AVE. JUNOT, 18TH ARR.
TEL 01 53 41 81 40
hotel-particulier-montmartre.com
This secluded retreat in a historic Montmartre mansion has five large rooms individually designed in a contemporary style and a walled garden with a fountain and shady corners.
5 Lamarck, Blanche
All major cards

■ B Montmartre
€€€
6 RUE LÉCLUSE, 17TH ARR.
TEL 01 42 93 35 77
FAX 01 42 94 19 08

b-montmartre.com
Nestled on a small street five minutes from Montmartre, this hotel has comfortable, stylishly decorated rooms and an exotic garden with palm trees.
36 Place de Clichy
All major cards

■ Terrass
€€€
12–14 RUE JOSEPH-DE-MAISTRE, 18TH ARR.
TEL 01 46 06 72 85
terrass-hotel.com
This large, 19th-century building has an art deco interior. The restaurant serves traditional French food.
98 Blanche, Place de Clichy
All major cards

■ Joséphine
€
67 RUE BLANCHE, 9TH ARR.
TEL 01 55 31 90 75
hotel-josephine.com
This hotel's colorful rooms feature black-and-white photos of 1920s cabaret dancers.
41 Blanche
All major cards

■ Regyn's Montmartre
€
18 PLACE DES ABBESSES, 18TH ARR.
TEL 01 42 54 45 21
FAX 01 42 59 08 85
www.paris-hotels-montmartre.com
Rooms are modern and quiet; those on the top floor have panoramic views of Paris.
22 Abbesses
All major cards

LANGUAGE **GUIDE**

GENERAL

Yes *Oui*
No *Non*
Excuse me *Excusez-moi*
Hello *Bonjour*
Hi *Salut*
Please *S'il vous plaît*
Thank you (very much) *Merci (beaucoup)*
You're welcome *De rien*
OK *D'accord*
Good bye *Au revoir*
Good night *Bonsoir*
Sorry *Pardon*
here *ici*
there *là*
today *aujourd'hui*
yesterday *hier*
tomorrow *demain*
this morning *ce matin*
this afternoon *cet aprés-midi*
this evening *ce soir*
Do you have . . . ? *Avez-vous . . . ?*
Do you speak English? *Parlez-vous anglais?*
I don't understand *Je ne comprends pas*
Please speak more slowly *Parlez plus lentement, s'il vous plaît*
Where is . . .? *Où est. . . ?*
I don't know *Je ne sais pas*
No problem *Ce n'est pas grave*
That's it *C'est ça*
Here it is *Voici*
There it is *Voilà*
What is your name? *Comment vous appellez-vous?*
My name is . . . *Je m'appelle . . .*
Let's go *On y va*
At what time? *À quelle heure?*
When? *Quand?*

In the Hotel

Do you have . . .? *Avez-vous . . . ?*
a single room *une chambre simple*
a double room *une chambre double*
with/without bathroom/ shower *avec/sans salle de bain/douche*

Help

I need a doctor/dentist *J'ai besoin d'un médecin/dentiste*
Can you help me? *Pouvez-vous m'aider?*
Where is the hospital? *Où est l'hôpital?*
Where is the police station? *Où est le commissariat?*

Shops

bakery *la boulangerie*
bookshop *la librairie*
delicatessen *la charcuterie/ le traiteur*
drugstore *la pharmacie*
fishmonger *la poissonnerie*
grocery *l'alimentation/l'épicerie*
supermarket *le supermarché*

Sightseeing

visitor information office *l'office de tourisme/le syndicat d'initiative*
open *ouvert*
closed *fermé*
every day *tous les jours*
year-round *toute l'année*
all day long *toute la journée*
free *gratuit/libre*
abbey *l'abbaye*
castle, country house *le château*
church *l'église*

museum *le musée*
staircase *l'escalier*
tower *la tour* (La Tour Eiffel)
tour (walk or drive) *le tour*

MENU READER

breakfast *le petit déjeuner*
lunch *le déjeuner*
dinner *le dîner*
I'd like to order *Je voudrais commander*
Is service included? *Est-ce que le service est compris?*

Le Menu

menu à prix fixe **meal at set price**
à la carte **dishes from the menu, charged separately**
entrée/hors d'oeuvre **first course**
le plat principal **main course**
le plat du jour **dish of the day**
le dessert **dessert**
boisson comprise **drink included**
carte des vins **wine list**
l'addition **the bill**

Les Boissons (Drinks)

café **coffee**
au lait ou crème **with milk or cream**
déca/décaféiné **decaffeinated coffee**
express/noir **espresso/black**
filtré **American filtered coffee**
thé **tea**
lait **milk**
gazeux **fizzy**
citron pressé **fresh lemon juice served with sugar**
orange pressée **fresh squeezed orange juice**
bière **beer**

INDEX

CREDITS

Walking Paris
Pas Paschali & Brian Robson

Since 1888, the National Geographic Society has funded more than 13,000 research, exploration, and preservation projects around the world. National Geographic Partners distributes a portion of the funds it receives from your purchase to National Geographic Society to support programs including the conservation of animals and their habitats.

National Geographic Partners
1145 17th Street NW
Washington, DC 20036-4688 USA

Get closer to National Geographic explorers and photographers, and connect with our global community. Join us today at
nationalgeographic.com/join

For information about special discounts for bulk purchases,
please contact National Geographic Books Special Sales:
specialsales@natgeo.com

For rights or permissions inquiries, please contact National
Geographic Books Subsidiary Rights: bookrights@natgeo.com

Edition edited by White Star s.r.l.
Licensee of National Geographic Partners, LLC.
Update by Iceigeo, Milan (Maria Chiara Piccolo, Alberto Brambilla, Nicola Bajetta, Cynthia Anne Koeppe)

The information in this book has been carefully checked and to the best of our knowledge is accurate. However, details are subject to change, and the publisher cannot be responsible for such changes, or for errors or omissions. Assessments of sites, hotels, and restaurants are based on the author's subjective opinions, which do not necessarily reflect the publisher's opinion.

ISBN: 978-88-544-1588-1

Printed by
Rotolito S.p.A. - Seggiano di Pioltello (MI) - Italy